Water Safety Plans: Book 1
Planning Water Safety Management for
Urban Piped Water Supplies
in Developing Countries

Water Safety Plans: Book 1

Planning Water Safety Management for Urban Piped Water Supplies in Developing Countries

Sam Godfrey & Guy Howard

Water, Engineering and Development Centre
Loughborough University
2005

Water, Engineering and Development Centre,
Loughborough University,
Leicestershire, LE11 3TU, UK

© WEDC, Loughborough University, 2005

ISBN 13 Paperback: 978 1 84380 052 1
ISBN Ebook: 9781788533713
Book DOI: http://dx.doi.org/10.3362/9781788533713

A catalogue record for this book is available from the British Library.

A reference copy of this publication is also available online at:
http://www.lboro.ac.uk/wedc/publications/

Godfrey, S. and Howard, G., (2005)
Water Safety Plans: Book 1
Planning Water Safety Management for
Urban Piped Water Supplies in Developing Countries
WEDC, Loughborough University, UK.

WEDC (The Water, Engineering and Development Centre) at Loughborough University in the UK is
one of the world's leading institutions concerned with education, training, research and consultancy
for the planning, provision and management of physical infrastructure for development in low- and
middleincome countries.

This edition is reprinted and distributed by Practical Action Publishing.
Since 1974, Practical Action Publishing has published and disseminated books and information
in support of international development work throughout the world. Practical Action Publishing
trades only in support of its parent charity objectives and any profits are covenanted back to
Practical Action (Charity Reg. No. 247257, Group VAT Registration No. 880 9924 76).

Designed at WEDC

About the authors

Sam Godfrey (sgodfrey@unicef.org) is currently working as a Water and Environmental Sanitation Project Officer and Technical Resource Officer for water quality with UNICEF in Bhopal, Madhya Pradesh, India. He is a Chartered Water and Environmental Manager with experience of risk assessment and management of both piped water supplies and groundwater in 15 countries in Africa, Asia and South America. He works for WEDC (the Water, Engineering and Development Centre), Loughborough University, UK where he has spent much of the last three years in Uganda and India researching appropriate risk assessment and management plans, which led to the production of these guidelines.

Dr Guy Howard (guyhoward@agni.com) is a DFID Infrastructure and Urban Development Advisor (from August 2003) and was previously a Programme Manager at WEDC, Loughborough University and Research Fellow at the Robens Centre for Public and Environmental Health, University of Surrey. He is a member of the Drinking Water Committee that oversees the revision of the WHO Guidelines for Drinking-Water Quality and is a co-author of the book Water Safety Plans: Managing drinking-water quality from catchment to consumer, which is the principal substantiation document on water safety plans for the WHO Guidelines.

Acknowledgements

The financial support of the UK Department for International Development (DFID) is gratefully acknowledged. The authors would also like to thank those who have contributed to the development of these guidelines.

Uganda

Sarah Tibatemwa, Chief Analyst, National Water & Sewerage Corporation (NWSC), Kampala
Charles Niwagaba, Department of Civil Engineering, Makerere University, Kampala
Frank Kizito, Geographical Information Section (GIS), NWSC, Kampala
Christopher Kanyesigye, Quality Control Manager, NWSC, Kampala
Alex Gisagara, Planning and Development Manager, NWSC, Kampala
Godfrey Arwata, Microbiologist, NWSC, Kampala,
Sekayizzi Andrew, Area Manager, NWSC, Jinja
Lillian Nabasirye, Area Engineer, NWSC, Jinja

India

Prem Chand, Md. Amwar, Venkateswara Rao, Rama Kumar
KAKTOS Consult, Hydrabad
Srinivas Chary, Administrative Staffing College of India (ASCI), Hydrabad
N.V.R.K. Prasada Rao, District Engineer, GMC, Guntur

United Kingdom and Europe

Professor Trudy Harpham and Dr Roger Few, South Bank University, London, UK
Dr Lorna Fewtrell, Centre for Research into Environment and Health, Wales
Dr Steve Pedley and Kali Johal, Robens, University of Surrey, UK
Oliver Schmoll, German Environment Agency, Germany
Dr Sam Kayaga and Kevin Sansom, WEDC, UK
Dr Margaret Ince, Consultant, UK

Finally, the authors wish to acknowledge Dr Kala Vairavamoorthy (WEDC) for his intellectual input and Sue Plummer and Karen Betts of the WEDC Publications Office.

Who should read this book

This book has been written specifically for practitioners involved in the operation, maintenance and management of piped water supplies in urban areas in developing countries.

These practitioners include engineers, water quality analysts, planners, managers, sociologists and water professionals involved in the monitoring and control of water safety in piped water supplies. The book is designed to provide guidance to operators of piped water supplies in urban areas on how to develop effective risk management plans, known as Water Safety Plans (WSPs). It is written exclusively to enable water suppliers to develop WSPs without having to depend heavily on specialized external input.

How to use this book

The book is designed to guide the user through the process of developing Water Safety Plans. It provides a simple step by step approach to developing WSPs for operators and managers of piped water supplies. At each stage, the principles of the stage are outlined as well as methods and tools required to achieve these principles. Each section ends with a summary of key competencies achieved from each stage.

How does this book fit into the overall guidelines?

This book is Document 1 in the guidelines series developed for Project KaR R8029, *Improved Risk Assessment and Management for Piped Urban Water Supplies*. It provides guidance on the practical aspects of water quality management in piped water supplies and outlines specific aspects of how to develop Water Safety Plans (WSP).

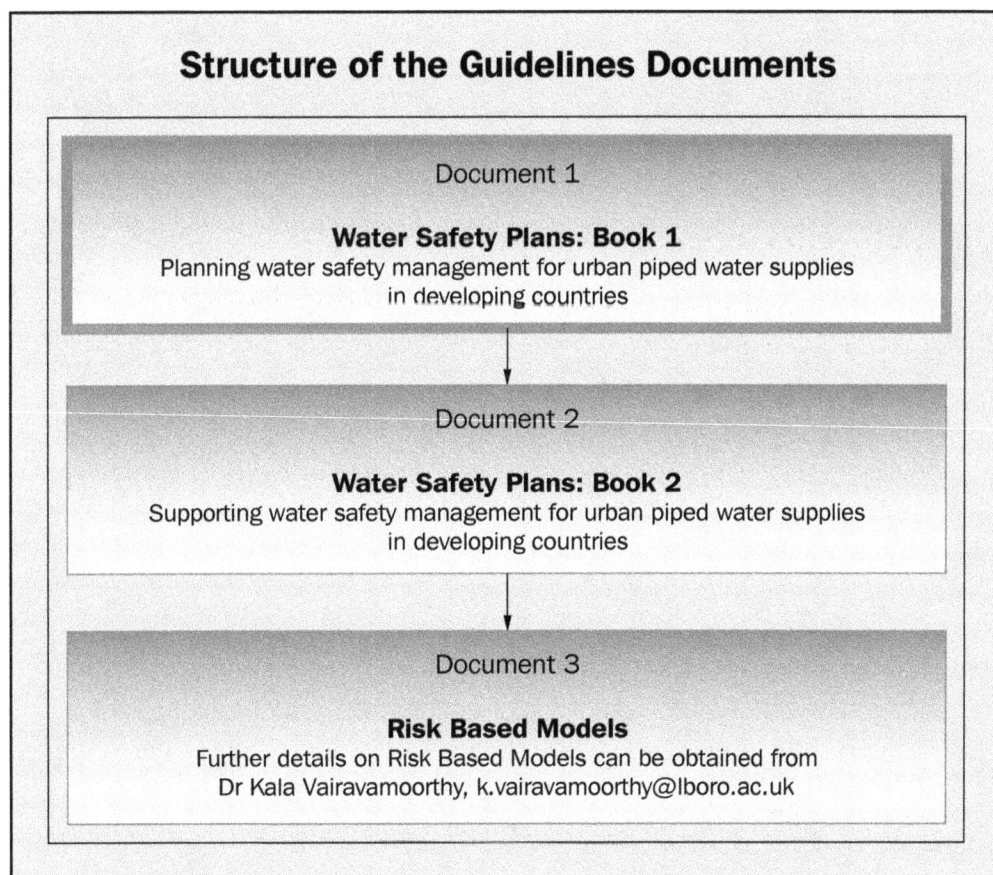

Structure of the Guidelines Documents

Document 1

Water Safety Plans: Book 1
Planning water safety management for urban piped water supplies in developing countries

Document 2

Water Safety Plans: Book 2
Supporting water safety management for urban piped water supplies in developing countries

Document 3

Risk Based Models
Further details on Risk Based Models can be obtained from Dr Kala Vairavamoorthy, k.vairavamoorthy@lboro.ac.uk

Contents

List of boxes

List of figures

List of acronyms

CD   Compact disc
GIS   Geographic Information System
GPS   Geographic Positioning System
HACCP   Hazard Assessment Critical Control Point
ISO   International Standards Office
NWSC   National Water and Sewerage Corporation
QCD   Quality Control Department
TQM   Total Quality Management
WHO   World Health Organization
WQA   Water Quality Assessment
WSP   Water Safety Plan

Flow chart key

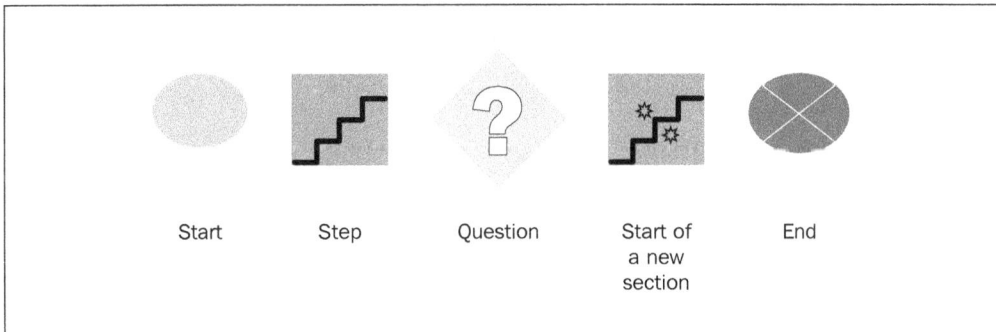

Start	Step	Question	Start of a new section	End

Chapter 1

Introduction

The delivery of safe drinking-water is vital for protecting public health and promoting more secure livelihoods in urban areas. Very often, however, assessment of water safety is limited to occasional tests of water quality and insufficient attention is paid to the proactive management of water safety.

To ensure the delivery of safe drinking-water, it is important that water safety objectives are established. These should take into account exposures and risk in order to make informed and balanced judgments about the levels of health protection required. Bartram et al. (2001), note that this process is cyclical, as shown in

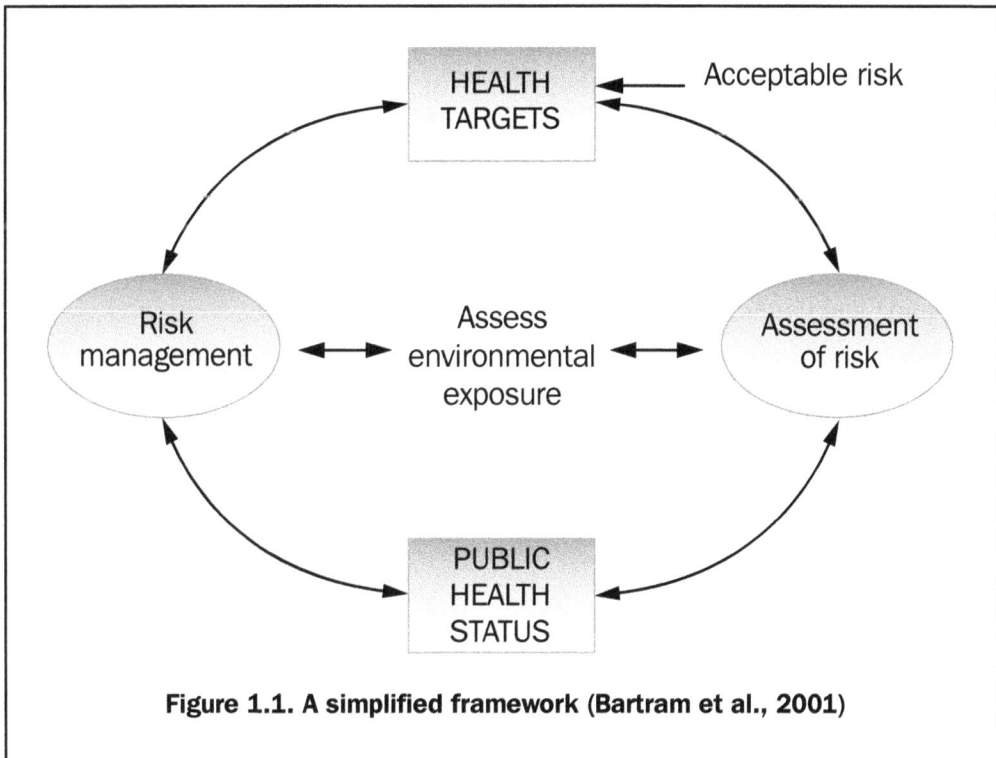

Figure 1.1. A simplified framework (Bartram et al., 2001)

Figure 1.1. In the revision of their *Guidelines for Drinking-Water Quality* the World Health Organization (WHO) identified five key components that are required to deliver safe drinking-water (WHO, 2004; Davison et al., 2004):

1. The establishment of **health-based targets** for microbial and chemical quality of water
2. A **system assessment** to determine whether the water supply chain from catchment to consumer can deliver safe drinking-water at the point of consumption
3. **Monitoring of identified control measures** within the water supply chain that provide assurance of safety
4. **Management plans** documenting the system assessment and monitoring and which describe the actions to be taken during normal operation and incident conditions to secure water safety
5. Independent public **health surveillance** of water safety

Steps 2 to 4 inclusive constitute what is called a Water Safety Plan (WSP). It is usually the responsibility of the water supplier to prepare, implement and evaluate the WSP. The establishment of health-based targets and surveillance are more typically the responsibility of the health sector (Havelaar et al., 2003; Howard, 2002; WHO, 1997; WHO, 2004).

This book is designed to help those staff in water supply agencies who are responsible for providing water through piped water systems to develop WSPs. The evidence presented, is the result of a three year Department for International Development (DFID) funded Knowledge and Research (KaR) project Contract No. R8029, *Improved risk assessment and management of piped urban water supplies*. Field research was undertaken in three project sites, Kampala and Jinja in Uganda and Guntur in Andrapradesh, India.

Extracts from each of these case studies are outlined in Annexe 2. Full details of the books can be obtained from WEDC, Loughborough University, UK or electronically at http://wedc.lboro.ac.uk/publications/index.htm

Why do we need WSPs?

The traditional approach to water quality and safety management has relied on the testing of drinking-water. This takes place as it leaves the treatment works or at selected points, either within the distribution system or at consumer taps. This is known as 'end-product testing'. The problem with this approach is that the results are too little and too late for preventative action. Figure 1.2 illustrates the intrinsic linkages between positive or negative testing of water quality, water collection and water-related health burdens.

Too little because so few samples are taken compared to the amount of water produced. Therefore, conclusions drawn about the safety of the water from the results of such sampling are inevitably compromised, particularly for microbial quality and in systems with a high throughput of water. Research has also shown that pathogens may be found when the commonly used indicator bacteria are not present and diseases can still be transmitted by water that meets standards for indicator bacteria (Payment, 1998, Medema, 2003).

Too late because usually by the time the results are available, the water has been supplied and may have been consumed and therefore preventive action is no longer possible. This is a particular problem in relation to microbial quality, where most tests provide quantitative results only after several hours of incubation.

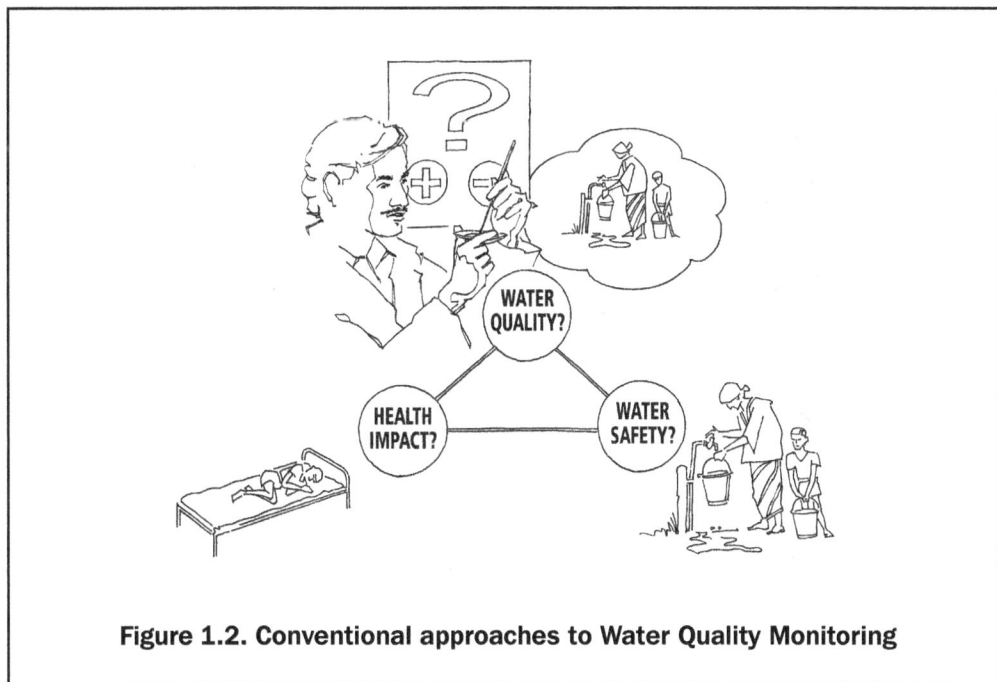

Figure 1.2. Conventional approaches to Water Quality Monitoring

Quality assurance

To improve the management of water safety, the use of quality assurance procedures is increasingly promoted (Deere et al., 2001, Davison et al., 2004, WHO, 2004). These quality assurance procedures have the advantage over end-product testing in that they ensure that the processes involved in delivering safe drinking-water are operated properly and under full control at all times. As these processes are designed to reduce, eliminate or prevent contamination of the water supply, when they are under control, so is the risk of contamination. When such approaches are adopted, monitoring can focus on simple, measured parameters. These rapidly identify where control is compromised, enabling action to be taken immediately to bring the system back into control before any contaminated water is distributed and consumed.

Quality assurance has been practised for many years in the water sector through the:

- multiple barrier principle in water supply design;
- documentation of operating procedures; and
- use of regular monitoring of key operational parameters such as chlorine residuals and turbidity.

Figure 1.3 outlines a conventional multiple barrier configuration showing raw water abstraction from a river, to water treatment, water storage, water distribution through pipes/valves and water collection at standpipes.

Some Northern water suppliers have applied formal quality assurance schemes such as those based on ISO 9000 and the Hazard Analysis and Critical Control Points (HACCP) scheme used in the food industry (Dillon, 1996). HACCP in particular has proved to be a valuable tool in ensuring the delivery of safe drinking-water and has been applied by a number of utility water supplies and within national risk management frameworks in Europe, the United States, Australia and New Zealand.

WSPs use many of the components of HACCP, but also elements of other approaches such as those within ISO 9000 and the concepts of total quality management (TQM). Although the use of a WSP provides greater assurance of quality and supports more effective asset management, they have not yet been widely applied in developing countries. One of the reasons for this is that 'crisis management' is the norm with many water suppliers in developing countries.

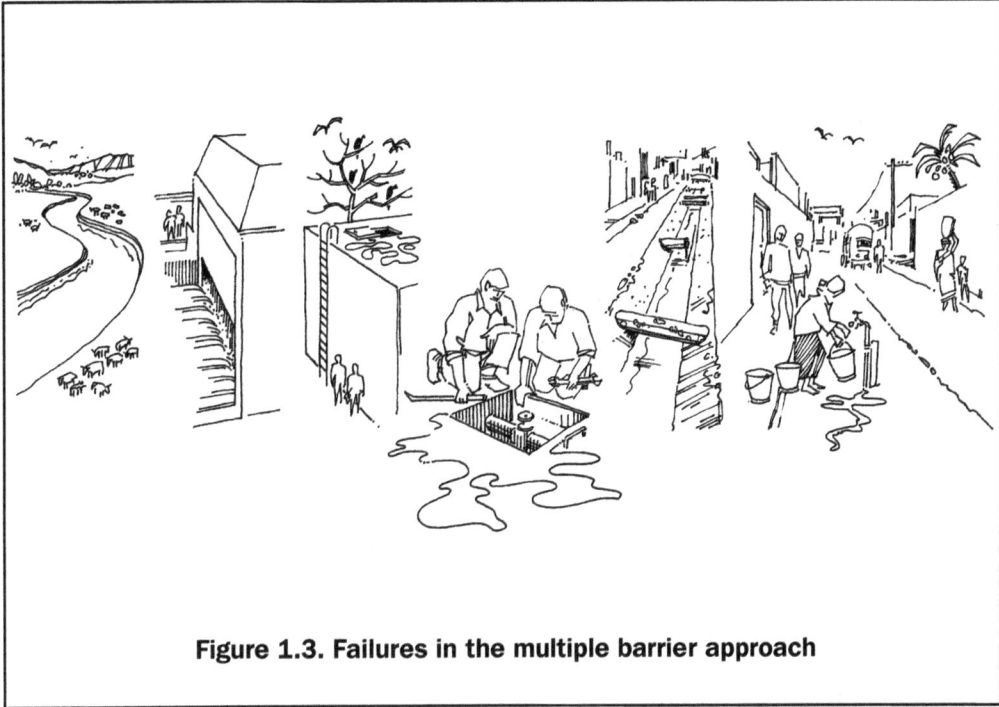

Figure 1.3. Failures in the multiple barrier approach

What is a Water Safety Plan?

A WSP is an improved risk management tool designed to ensure the delivery of safe drinking-water. It identifies:

- the hazards that the water supply is exposed to and the level of risk associated with each;
- how each hazard will be controlled;
- how the means of control will be monitored;
- how the operator can tell if control has been lost;
- what actions are required to restore control; and
- how the effectiveness of the whole system can be verified.

By developing a WSP, the system managers and operators will gain a thorough understanding of their system and the risks that must be managed. This knowledge can then be used to develop operational plans and identify key priorities for action. The development of a WSP will also identify what additional training and capacity-building initiatives are required to support and improve the performance of the water supplier in meeting water safety targets.

How to develop a Water Safety Plan

The development of a Water Safety Plan involves:

- preventing contamination of source waters;
- treating water to reduce or remove contamination in order that water safety targets are met; and
- preventing re-contamination during storage, distribution and handling of water.

In order to do this, the water supplier needs to:

- assemble a team that understands the system and its ability to meet the water quality targets;
- identify where contamination could arise within the water supply, and how it could be controlled;
- validate the methods employed to control hazards;
- establish both a monitoring system to check that safe water is consistently supplied and agreed corrective actions in the case of deviation outside acceptable limits; and
- periodically verify that the Water Safety Plan is being implemented correctly and is achieving the performance required to meet the water safety targets.

To establish a WSP, a number of steps are required. There are some essential prerequisites, such as getting commitment from managers and relevant planning activities. Once this commitment has been gained, the WSP steering group is formed, the water supply system described, field assessments of the supply undertaken and then system-specific WSP matrices developed that can be periodically improved and verified using selected microbial parameters.

Figure 1.4 outlines the main steps in developing a WSP, all of which are described in this book.

This project developed at the same time that the WHO *Guidelines for Drinking-Water Quality* (GDWQ) Edition 3 was being revised. Water Safety Plans by Davison et al. (2004) is a critical supporting document to the development of the WHO GDWQ 2004. This book has some similarities in approach to the methods of developing a WSP outlined in that book. However, this book describes findings from developing and implementing WSPs in developing countries. The approaches required are different for the following selected reasons:

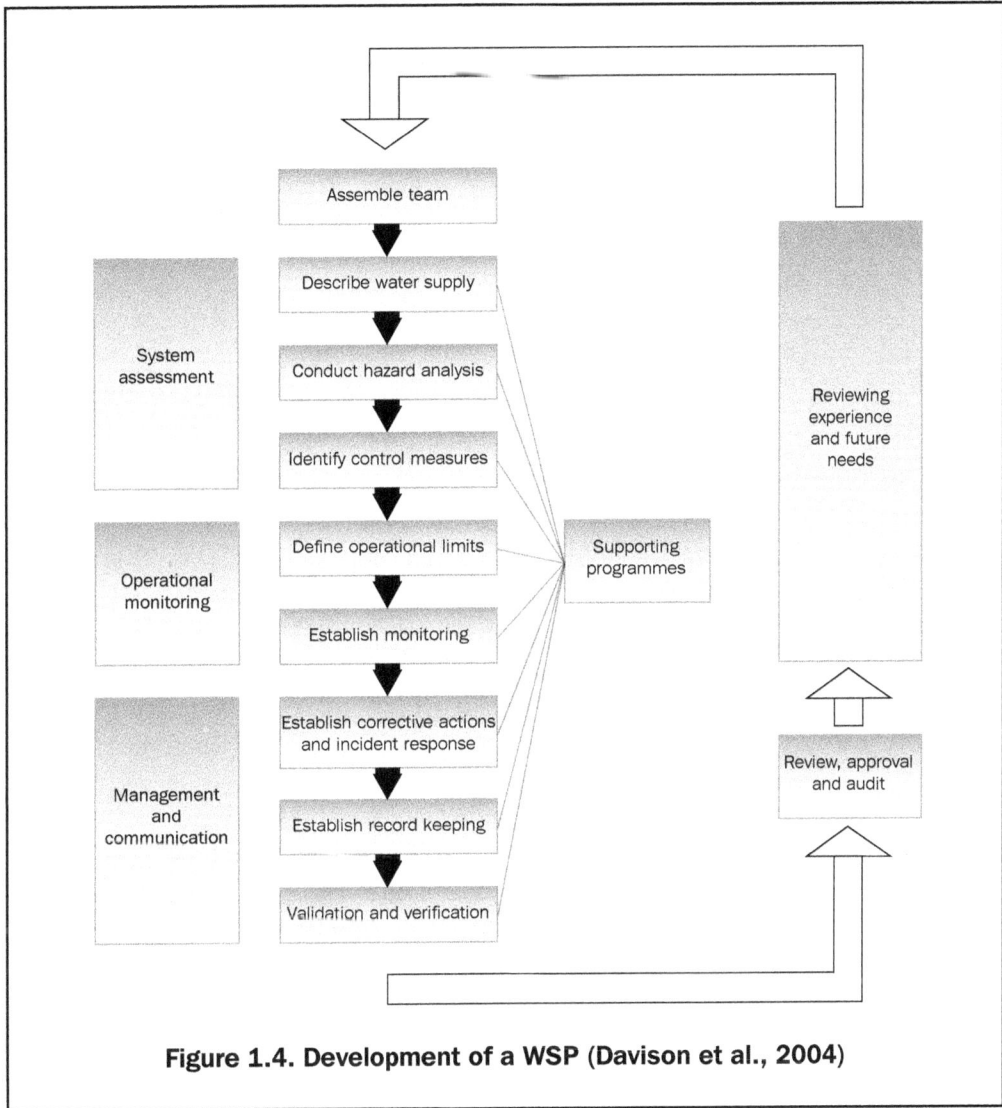

Figure 1.4. Development of a WSP (Davison et al., 2004)

1. Limited data availability – many systems in the developing world are only recently developing the culture of data collection and storage.
2. Unplanned development – limited regulation has resulted in unplanned development making it difficult to locate all supply mains.
3. Sanitation – poor access to urban sanitation means potential cross contamination of water pipes is common.
4. System knowledge – much of the information on the piped networks may not be available as records may have been removed by contractors, colonial powers.
5. Equipment/human resource availability – selection of appropriate water quality parameters should consider availability of resources.

Because of these factors, this project developed a more concise approach to developing WSPs for developing countries. The principles remain the same as those outlined in Davison et al. (2004) but include specific refinements and different terminology. For example, in Uganda significant time was spent in locating the pipelines during a desk-based system analysis stage before any form of system assessment could be undertaken. Because up-to-date network maps are rarely available, the system analysis may involve heavy reliance on expert judgement (i.e. local knowledge).

Figure 1.5 outlines the key steps required when developing WSPs in developing countries.

Commitment from managers and operational staff

Before the process of developing the WSP, it is imperative that all members of the water supplier agree on the benefits. Technical staff need a commitment to the WSP approach from all management levels, from field managers to the managing director. This section outlines examples of appropriate ways to achieve this agreement from the different groups and emphasizes the importance of obtaining commitment from all levels of staff. It further highlights that different tools and approaches are recommended for different groups of staff. The section is divided into *management* commitment and *operational* commitment.

For successful implementation of the WSP, it is important that senior management buy into the process. This process is crucial to obtain support for changes in working practices and to actively promote water safety as a goal of the organization.

It is key to obtain a commitment from senior management so that clear and coherent arguments can be presented which explain why the adoption of a WSP is necessary and advantageous to the organisation, and why a WSP is preferable to other approaches. Therefore, it is important to outline:

- what is being done now;
- where the organization wants to be in the future; and,
- how the organization aims to get there.

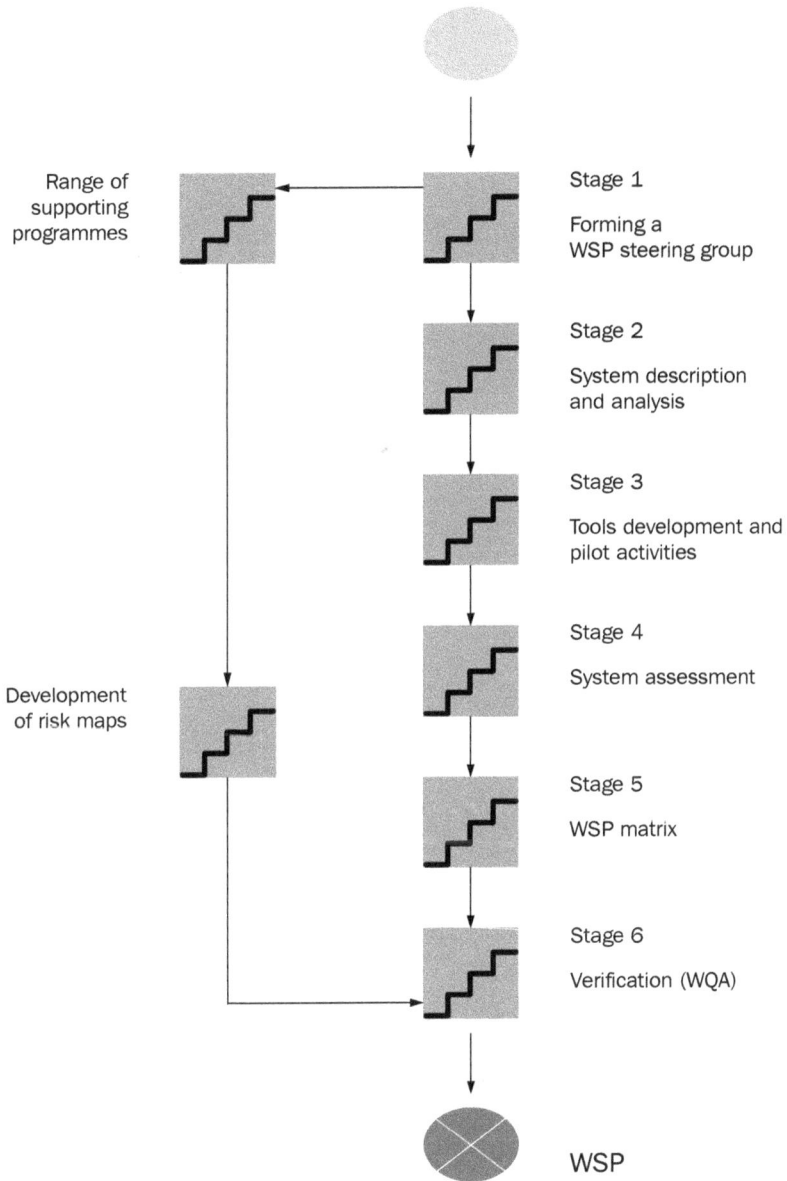

Figure 1.5. Developing WSPs in developing countries

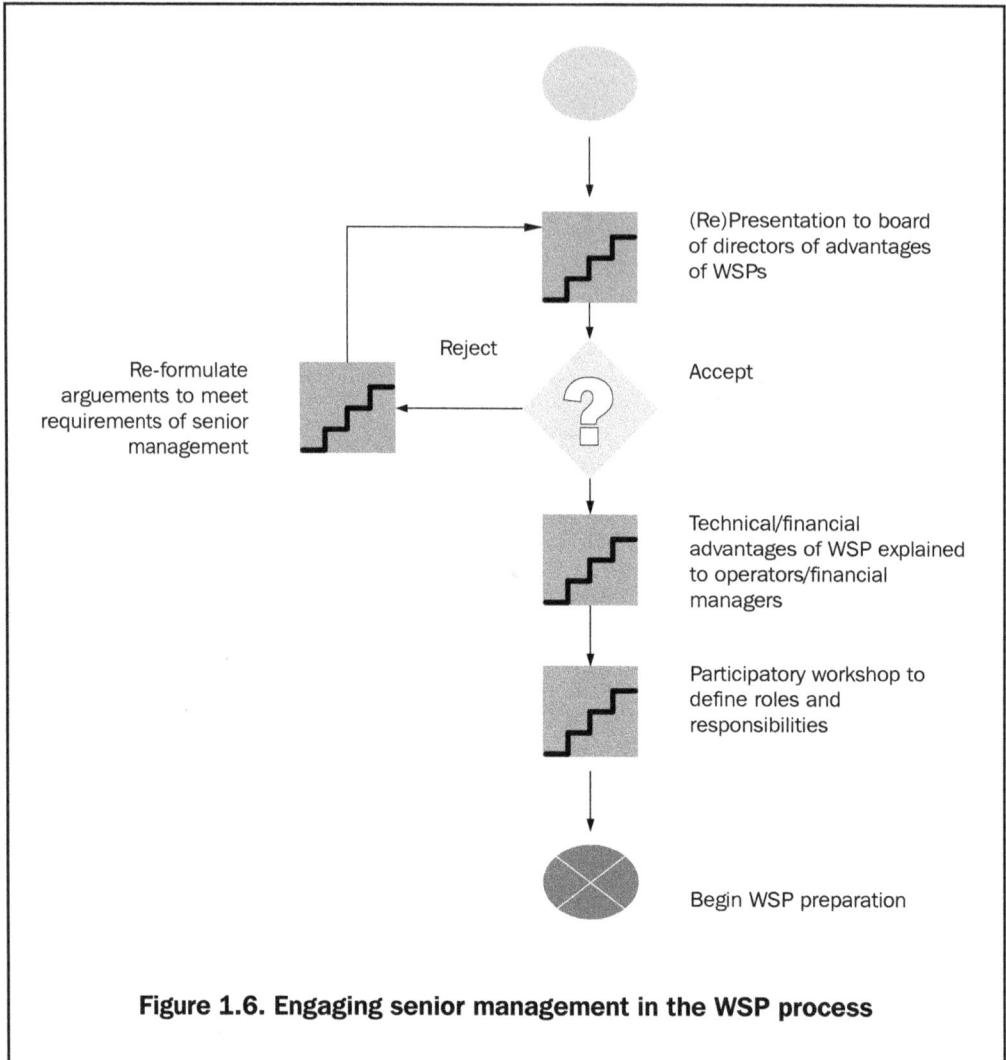

Figure 1.6. Engaging senior management in the WSP process

Figure 1.6 outlines some suggested ways to engage senior management in the WSP process. The strategy to obtain management commitment to the WSP process must fit within a broader planning process. This should consider the wider financial and resource implications of undertaking a WSP instead of conventional water quality monitoring. Central to this is the process of emphasizing in non-scientific terms the advantages of WSPs (such as cost savings and appropriateness of quality assurance approaches rather than quality control). For example, it was estimated that the Ugandan National Water and Sewerage Corporation (NWSC) saved 30 per cent in their total budget for water quality control by implementing a WSP instead of conventional water quality monitoring (Howard, in press).

Management commitment

The first stage in achieving management commitment to the WSP process is to prepare a short briefing note or proposal on the WSP approach. This may include the WSP benefits, what current activities undertaken by the utility are consistent with the WSP approach, what new working practices may be required and what will be the expected impacts on cost.

During the initial meeting with utility board of directors and operations managers, it is important to present the briefing note to the senior management team. In this presentation, emphasis should be placed on why the WSP approach is appropriate. The actual approach adopted will vary according to the specific environment within which the water supplier is operating. Different aspects of the WSP will be attractive to managers in different circumstances. A range of possible key entry points are noted below:

- WSPs are cutting-edge approaches that demonstrate to the public, health bodies and regulators that the water supplier is applying best practice to secure water safety;
- Quality assurance can secure water safety;
- There are limitations to relying on end-product testing as a means of water safety control;
- There is potential for savings with the WSP approach;
- There is potential to market services to new and existing consumers of an improved product.

The briefing should also outline how the WSP could be implemented, for instance, by proposing a pilot project be initiated on one supply as a means of demonstrating the feasibility of the WSP approach. This will probably include running the pilot project alongside existing water quality management as a means of evaluating WSP feasibility. This approach may gain greater acceptance as it does not imply an immediate change to a WSP and will provide senior managers with evidence from their own supplies to review before committing to a change in operating practice.

The further technical, scientific and financial advantages of the WSP can be presented in full once an initial consultation has been undertaken. An example of the format that this presentation could take is outlined in Box 1.1.

Box 1.1. Management buy in – NWSC Kampala, Uganda

An initial briefing meeting was held in the NWSC Kampala headquarters with NWSC's Managing Director, senior managers, engineers and accountants as well as, analysts from the Water Quality Control Department, and operators from both the water distribution and sewer networks.

A presentation was given by technical staff and covered the following topics:

1. Current water quality monitoring practise
2. Weaknesses in end-product testing in comparison to the Water Safety Plan (WSP) approach
3. How to establish WSPs
4. Advantages/disadvantages of the WSP approach (financial, technical)
5. The benefits of piloting the WSP approach.

The key output needed from the senior management meeting and briefing note is approval for the implementation of a WSP pilot project and a commitment that the outcomes of this pilot will determine whether full-scale adoption of the WSP will occur. This is the approach that was followed in Uganda (Godfrey et al., 2004). It allowed the water quality control department to make a case at each stage of WSP development for further activities and resulted in WSP definition being included in work plans.

Operational commitment

A WSP can only be successfully introduced if there is commitment from operational staff. So, the in-house promotion of WSPs is vital. The job descriptions of water treatment plant operators, plumbers, water quality monitors and analysts vary greatly. In some small systems one or two individuals are responsible for all of these tasks, whereas, in larger systems a team of ten or more people may be responsible for each of the jobs.

It is important to ensure that this commitment is developed in parallel with the development of the WSP itself. A meeting needs to be held with staff to present and discuss WSPs in relation to existing practice and to review the features of WSPs that make it a more effective way of ensuring water safety.

One important aspect of this process is to show the interlinkages between the role of the different job descriptions. This must be explained in language that is understandable at a local level. The use of decision trees such as those described in Box 1.2 can help to explain the interlinkages.

Box 1.2. WSP interlinkages

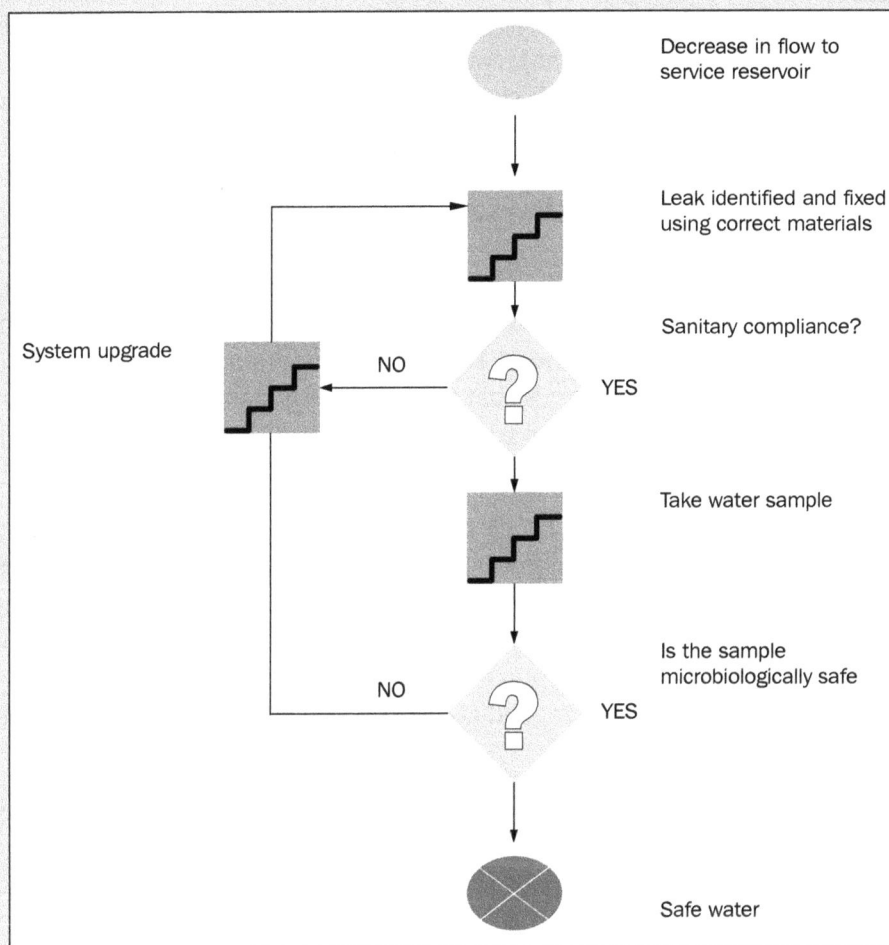

Decrease in flow to service reservoir

Leak identified and fixed using correct materials

Sanitary compliance?

System upgrade

NO

YES

Take water sample

Is the sample microbiologically safe

NO

YES

Safe water

Example

The service reservoir attendant records a decrease in flow into the service reservoir and so contacts the distribution engineer to check if any leaks have developed in the network. A leak is identified at a valve on the transmission main and a maintenance team is called out to fix the leaking valve box. Whilst fixing the leaking valve, they realise that they do not have the recommended Teflon tape. Instead plastic is wrapped around the pipe that connects to the valve. The following day, the water quality analyst notes deterioration in microbial quality because there is both no free chlorine and an increase in turbidity and so conducts a sanitary inspection which identifies the problem. The analyst immediately informs the operations department and initiates action. The analyst takes a sample for microbial analysis, which shows that because he acted promptly, the risk to public health was greatly reduced.

The example in Box 1.2 shows that if the analyst had relied solely on the results of the microbiological analysis before taking action there would have been a greater risk to public health; ongoing contamination would have occurred. Box 1.2 also stresses the importance of the interlinkages between the roles of different operations staff. For the WSP approach to function, clear job descriptions on roles and responsibilities for each staff member should be established. In many cases, the roles will not vary considerably from existing practices. For example, the only variation may be in the level of detailed reporting required and type of data collected and disseminated by each section.

When initiating discussions with operational staff to obtain their commitment to WSPs, it is important to discuss fully and frankly the concerns they may have about changes in working practices. It is important to emphasize that in many situations, actual working practices change very little under a WSP. Consequently, tasks already undertaken as part of routine activity may become more formal.

How is a WSP different?

WSPs will increase the amount of time staff spend in the field inspecting the system and undertaking physio-chemical analysis and *reduce* reliance on analysing samples of water for micro-organisms in a laboratory, as shown in Box 1.3. Crucially, the WSP enables the operators to get to know their system more effectively as they spend more time identifying and controlling risks rather than just analysing them.

Planning

Once there is agreement that the WSP approach will be piloted, it is important to develop a plan of activity and to identify which organizations and staff will undertake particular roles within the WSP.

Undertaking an organizational and institutional review

In many cases, it will be useful to review the current organizational and institutional structure of the water supplier and other sector stakeholders in order to establish which organizations have an interest in and/or responsibility for water safety. These should be undertaken in two stages to deal with both the internal and external environments. The internal environment is the operating environment of the water supplier and the external environment is the other organizations or groups and consumers involved or interested in water safety.

Box 1.3. Advantages of WSPs

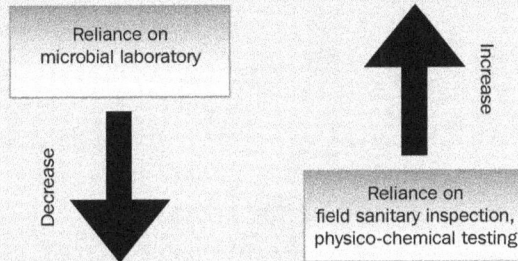

Reliance on
microbial laboratory

Decrease

Increase

Reliance on
field sanitary inspection,
physico-chemical testing

The first stage in this process is to prepare a list of all the departments within the water supplier. Each department should be asked to identify what their role is with regard to water safety, the number of staff in their department, the level and nature of work carried out, the position of the head in relation to management and the head of department's influence over decisions regarding water safety. Then an activity-responsibility matrix can be developed and roles within the WSP can be allocated to the different departments and units.

A review should also be undertaken of the roles, responsibilities and interests in water safety of external stakeholders. This review should address statutory roles, all aspects of regulation (financial, safety, environment), involvement in capital and operational investment in specific circumstances (for instance epidemics), and interest groups. For each stakeholder, the relative influence each has over policy, investment, regulation and operations should be noted as a means of identifying how each stakeholder interacts with the supplier. It is important to note that in undertaking this exercise, all stakeholders should be identified and not only those who are of power or influence. For instance, consumers may not be powerful, but they are the most important stakeholders.

Once the stakeholder analysis has been completed, an activity-responsibility matrix for the sector stakeholders can be developed as a means of understanding the institutional environment within which water safety operates. This will help guide the subsequent implementation of the WSP.

Planning activities

It is recommended that a transparent management plan for the implementation of the WSP is designed. To aid this process, GANTT charts or other methods of project-line management may be used in the initial project planning stage (see Box 1.4). DFID's *Guidance Manual for Water Supply and Sanitation Programmes* (1998) provides a useful reference for management models.

When designing the GANTT chart, it is important to calculate the number of person days required for the principal activities needed to implement the WSP. It should be stressed that there is no standard for the number of days required to undertake each activity or a standard number of times each activity is required. Both of these decisions are specific to the water supply. For example, undertaking the field assessment of a large water distribution system of more than 800km of pipeline in Kampala took 40 person days, while the assessment of a smaller network in Guntur of 600km took 15 days.

The final activity is a verification exercise using selected microbial parameters. It is recommended that this is undertaken once the WSP has been developed for the individual supply. In the context of this research, the exercise required 5 person days in the Guntur supply and 20 working days in the Kampala supply. Subsequently a rolling programme of verification testing should be established once the WSP is operational in order to test the effectiveness of the plan in improving water safety within the supply.

Outlined in the following sections are details of the major steps in establishing the WSP. They follow the seven major stages developed during this research for effective implementation of WSPs in developing countries and conclude with principles on how to implement the WSP once completed.

Box 1.4. GANTT chart of activities

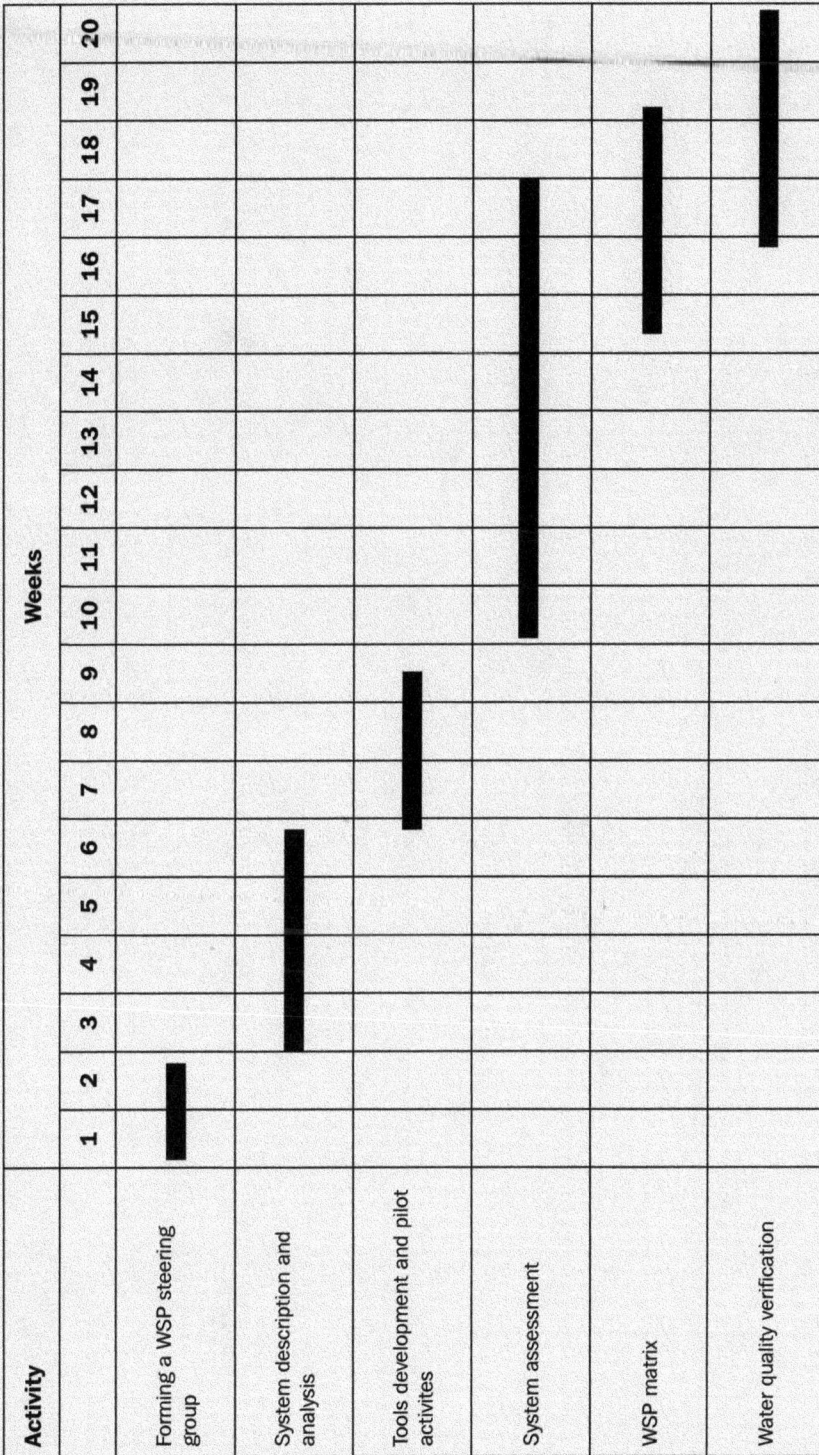

Activity	Weeks																			
	1	2	3	4	5	6	7	8	9	10	11	12	13	14	15	16	17	18	19	20
Forming a WSP steering group		█																		
System description and analysis			█		█	█														
Tools development and pilot activites							█	█	█											
System assessment										█	█	█	█				█			
WSP matrix															█	█	█	█	█	
Water quality verification																█	█	█	█	█

Chapter 2

Stage 1: Forming a WSP steering group

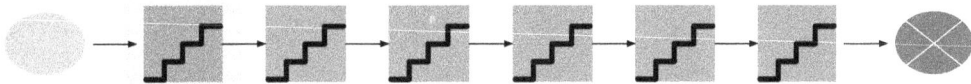

Stage 1	Stage 2	Stage 3	Stage 4	Stage 5	Stage 6
Forming a WSP steering group	System description and analysis	Tools development and pilot activities	System assessment	WSP matrix	Verification (WQA)

A steering group should be set up to guide the process of implementing a WSP. It is recommended that this is composed of members from varied professional backgrounds in order to form a balanced interdisciplinary team. As well as engineers and water quality managers, the steering group may include academics, planners, surveyors, sociologists and health scientists. The balance of varied professionals is important to ensure that the water safety plan incorporates financial, technical and social considerations.

During the process of forming the WSP steering group, it is important to identify a risk manager. The risk manager has overall responsibility for establishing the WSP.

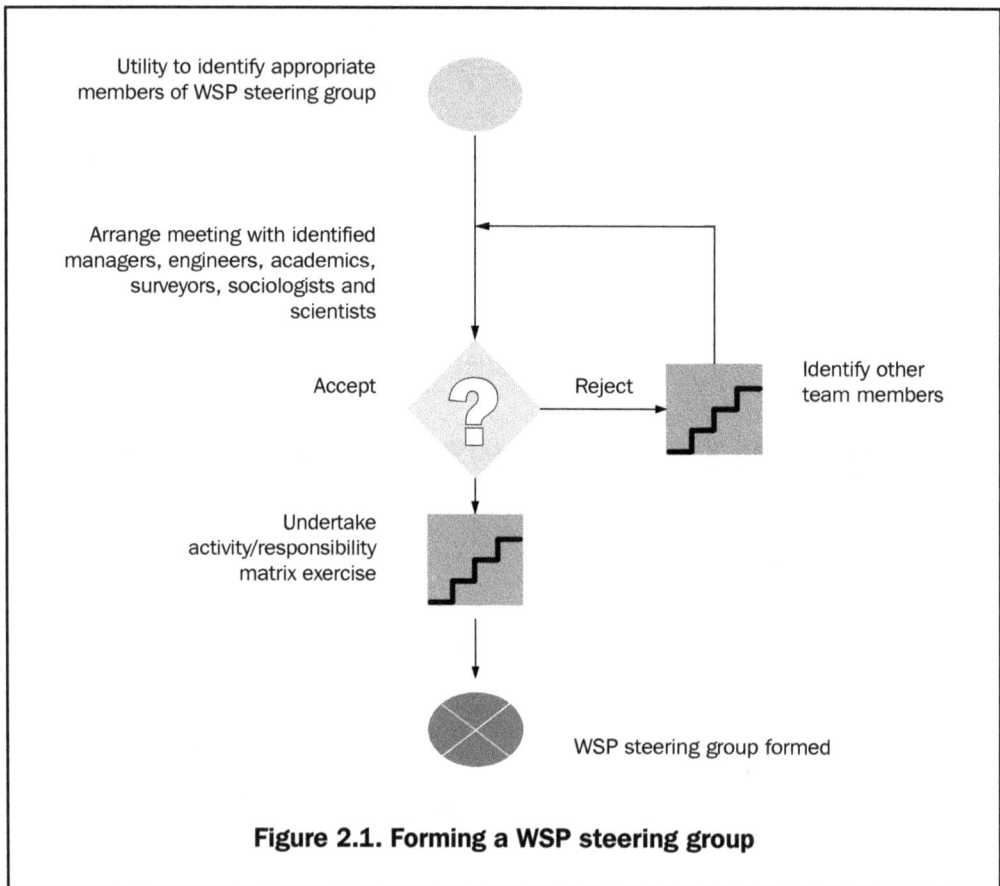

Figure 2.1. Forming a WSP steering group

Box 2.1. Forming a WSP steering group in Kampala

In Kampala, the WSP steering group was formed during initial discussions with the senior management of NWSC. Members of the team were selected on the basis of their professional ability as well as the extent of their involvement in water safety related activities. Most people volunteered to be members of the team during a consultation meeting with the Managing Director of the National Water and Sewerage Corporation (NWSC). These volunteers were from NWSC and academia (Public Health and Environmental Engineering Laboratory of Makerere University).

As NWSC are responsible for water quality, the team was co-ordinated by the NWSC WQCD. The Principal Analyst of NWSC WQCD was appointed as the risk manager.

In allocating specific tasks in the preparation and implementation of the WSP, an activity-responsibility matrix should be used to assign specific responsibilities to individual members of the task force. Box 2.2 outlines how this can be done for two important activities in setting up WSPs; the system assessment and the water quality assessment.

Box 2.2. Activity/responsibility matrix

Activity/ responsibility	Task force members					
	Principle water quality analysis	Senior engineers	Chief engineer	Operations manager	Quality control manager	Health department
System assessment	I	R	A	A	A	A
Water quality assessment	R	I	A	I	A	A

Where
I = Involved   R = Responsible   A = Aware

It is important to divide responsibilities amongst the stakeholders during the assessment stage. This division must receive full approval from senior managers. This is achieved by ensuring that the core of the WSP steering group are middle and/or senior managers. These staff should have a broad understanding of the use of a WSP as a means of improving water quality in their water supply.

Chapter 3

Stage 2: System description and analysis

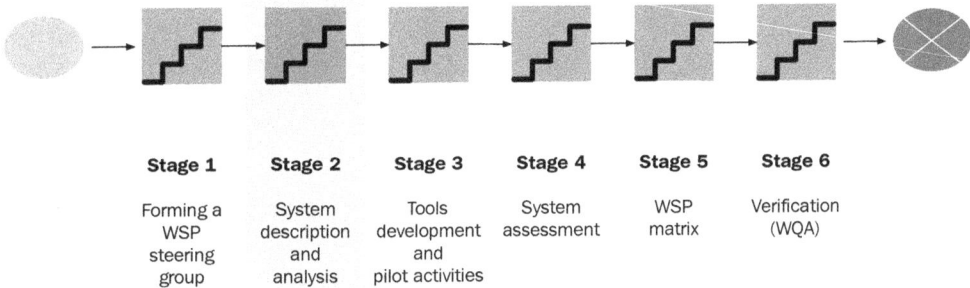

Stage 1	Stage 2	Stage 3	Stage 4	Stage 5	Stage 6
Forming a WSP steering group	System description and analysis	Tools development and pilot activities	System assessment	WSP matrix	Verification (WQA)

In developing the WSP, it is essential to ensure that the members of the team have a good understanding of how the water supply is designed and operated, and the nature of the people that are served by the supply. The first stage is therefore to develop a description of the system, which may be supported by a basic flow diagram for the supply. Next, the intended use of the water and vulnerability level assessment of the varied end-user groups should be defined.

The description of the water supply should include the:

- source of water and catchment (for instance capacity of the source in relation to demand, protection measures applied, developments in the catchment that may affect quality, known water quality problems)
- treatment processes applied (providing information about configurations, numbers of individual units, age of plant, known design faults)
- storage within the distribution systems (how many service reservoirs, their volume, areas that they serve, age, known design problems)
- distribution system (limit of responsibility of utility, extent, population served, known problems); and,
- consideration of re-contamination in household distribution and/or storage

An example of an overview water supply description from Guntur, India is outlined in Box 3.1.

Box 3.1. Water supply description – Guntur, India

The Guntur system is fed from surface water extracted from the river Krishna. It has two treatment works using conventional treatment unit processes (coagulation/flocculation/sedimentation/chlorination). The combined capacity of the works is $75,000m^3$ per day which is then distributed to service reservoirs. The Guntur Municipal Corporation (operators of the network) supplies $66,363m^3$ per day from the service reservoirs through 21 elevated tanks and 10 ground level tanks. The city is divided into 10 zones and the water is distributed through 600km of pipeline.

Describing the catchment and treatment processes should be relatively easy as data is known or can be readily acquired. When undertaking the preliminary system analysis, it is worth reviewing the data available to evaluate the likely source-water contaminant loads. For treatment processes, the literature can be consulted to identify expected log reductions through individual treatment processes. This can be used as a guide to whether these will provide sufficient removal in relation to expected source-water loads. One good source of information is a review by LeChevallier and Au (2003). Where there is very little data on source water quality, use the estimates of source water contamination provided in the WHO *Guidelines for Drinking-Water Quality* (WHO, 2004).

At this stage, it is also useful to prepare a diagram showing the flow of water through the treatment works, identifying each unit process and the location of principal inlets, flow control valves and dosing pumps as well as valves, backwashing tanks, etc. Box 3.2 outlines an example of the treatment configuration in Kampala, Uganda.

This configuration gives a breakdown of the main treatment unit processes and the location of the principal pumps and meters. The location of the isolation and sluice valves is not included in order to keep this stage of the summary simple. Once a thorough understanding of the source, catchment and treatment of the supply has been established, it is important to summarize the system as a whole, indicating the location of the service reservoirs and the general configuration of the distribution system, before providing a detailed description of the distribution system. This initial description can be summarized in the form of a simple flow chart as shown in Box 3.3.

Once a detailed system description has been undertaken, an initial assessment can be made to ascertain if the water supply can, at least in principle, supply drinking-water to within safe limits. This stage is critical as it determines whether there will be a need for investment in infrastructure in order to deliver safe drinking-water. For instance, if the water source is heavily contaminated surface water with seasonally high turbidity loads and the only treatment applied is rapid sand filtration and terminal disinfection, it is unlikely that safe drinking-water can be assured. By contrast, the same source treated with coagulation, flocculation, settling, rapid sand filtration and chlorination could assure safe drinking-water.

Even where investment needs are identified, it is important to first put in place the components of the WSP that can be implemented without investment. This provides greater confidence that the water produced is as safe as can be achieved with current resources.

Box 3.2. Water treatment – Gaba 11, Kampala, Uganda

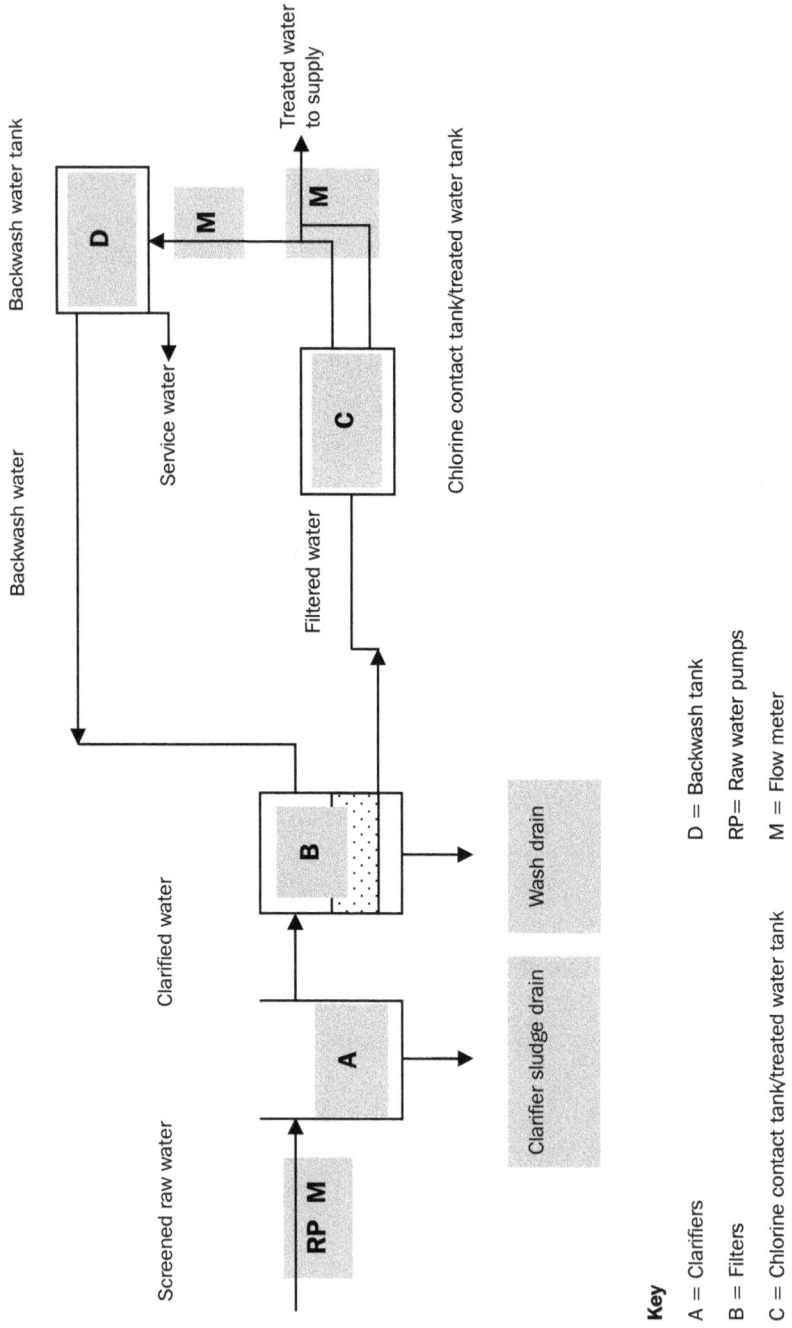

Screened raw water

RP M

Clarified water

A

Clarifier sludge drain

B

Wash drain

Backwash water

Service water

Filtered water

Chlorine contact tank/treated water tank

C

M

M

D

Backwash water tank

Treated water to supply

Key

A = Clarifiers
B = Filters
C = Chlorine contact tank/treated water tank

D = Backwash tank
RP= Raw water pumps
M = Flow meter

Box 3.3. Flow diagram of water supply – Guntur, India

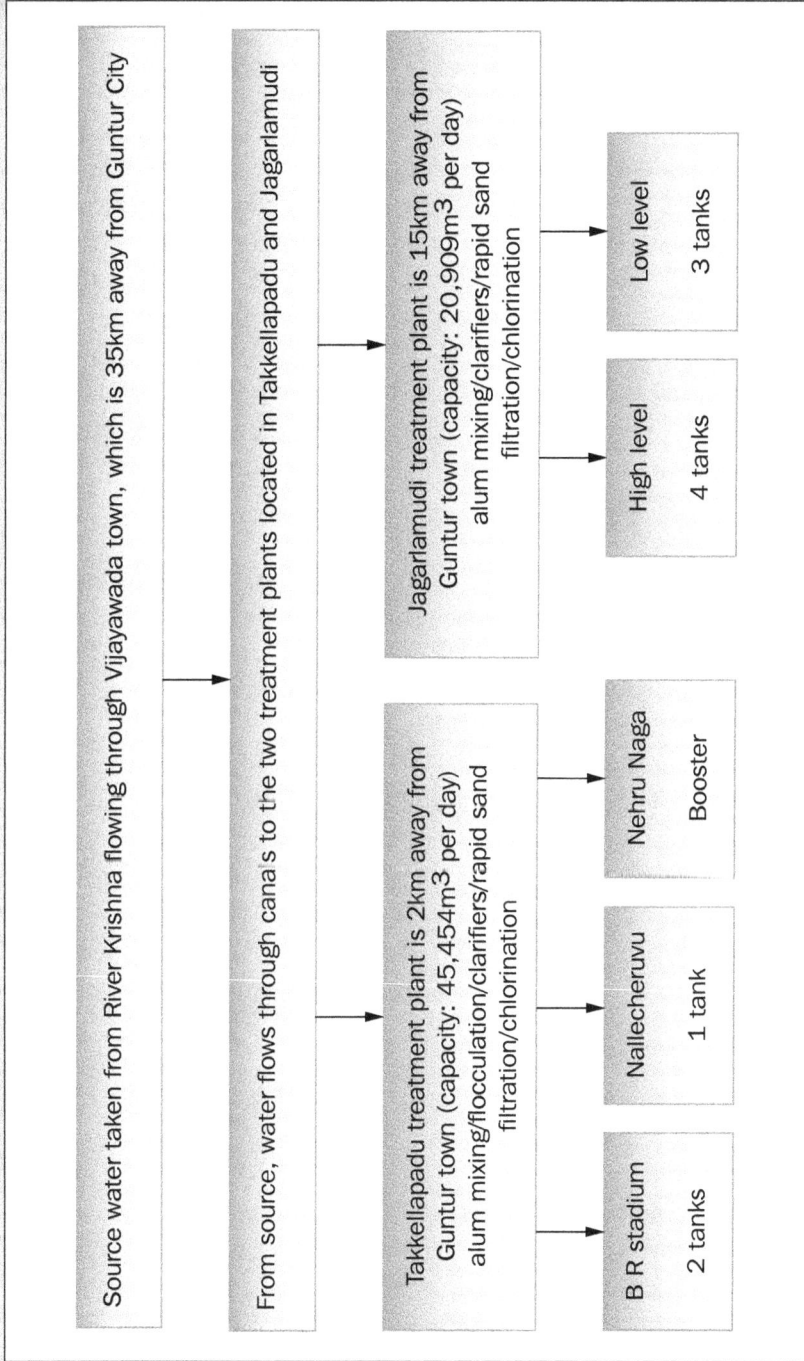

Source water taken from River Krishna flowing through Vijayawada town, which is 35km away from Guntur City

From source, water flows through canals to the two treatment plants located in Takkellapadu and Jagarlamudi

Takkellapadu treatment plant is 2km away from Guntur town (capacity: 45,454m³ per day) alum mixing/flocculation/clarifiers/rapid sand filtration/chlorination

Jagarlamudi treatment plant is 15km away from Guntur town (capacity: 20,909m³ per day) alum mixing/clarifiers/rapid sand filtration/chlorination

B R stadium

2 tanks

Nallecheruvu

1 tank

Nehru Naga

Booster

High level

4 tanks

Low level

3 tanks

Describing the distribution system

Assessing the distribution system may prove more challenging than water treatment works and catchments was with regard to description and preliminary analysis. It will require a particular understanding of the hydraulics of the system, the materials, age and size of the pipes and the location of the water supply pipes in relation to areas where hazards exist. Therefore, the departments undertaking monitoring and those responsible for water operation must share their knowledge of existing trends in water quality and hydraulic patterns within the network that might result in intermittence, discontinuity or pressure waves in supply. By drawing this information together in the system analysis, the WSP steering group can identify 'problem spots' susceptible to contamination within the network.

Start by undertaking a preliminary desk-based analysis of the entire distribution network. The flow diagram in Figure 3.1 outlines the steps involved in analysing the distribution system and shows how each step links to the overall objective of establishing a Water Safety Plan.

During the desk-based assessment, the condition and details of the main service reservoirs or supply tanks within the water supply system should be noted. This should include a brief assessment of the physical condition of the distribution system. This can be assessed by analysing the condition of the pipe. Key indicators of pipe condition that could be considered are:

- Pipe age – the effects of pipe degradation becomes more apparent over time
- Pipe diameter – small diameter pipes are more susceptible to beam failure
- Pipe length and jointing - long water pipes are more susceptible to longitude breaks
- Pipe material – assess vulnerability of pipe to failure based on combination of hydraulic pressure exerted on the pipe and corrosivity of soil in which pipe is laid

Full details and justification for the selection of these indicators can be found in this series.

As well as the pipe network, the service reservoirs, supply tanks and major valves should also be assessed, including percentage level of sanitary risk associated with each facility. For example, findings from an initial assessment in Guntur, India revealed that 50 per cent of the supply tanks were of concern in the provision of safe drinking-water (see details in Box 3.4).

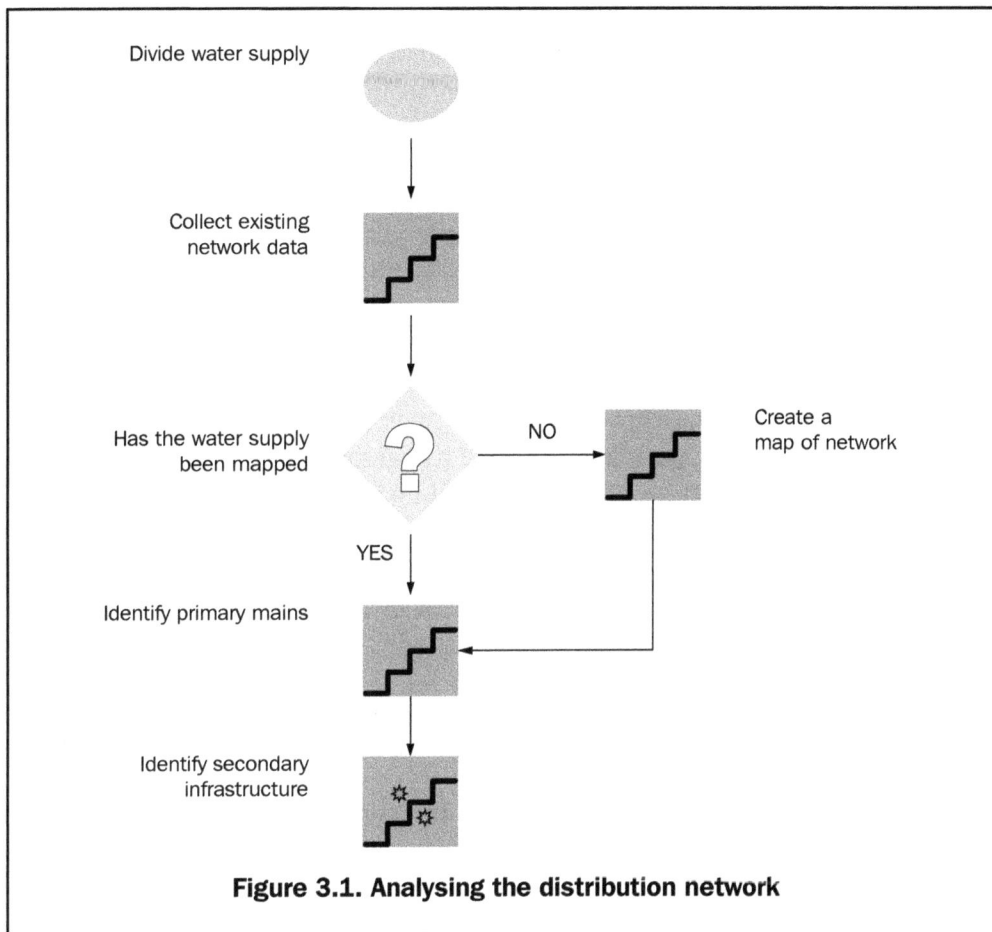

Figure 3.1. Analysing the distribution network

Box 3.4. Supply tank detail

Name of the area and tank	No. of tanks	Age	Zone	Capacity (m³)	Condition
B R Stadium	2	18	VIII	2,960	BAD

Additional information recorded: air vents were not covered due to broken mesh on vents, inspection covers were highly corroded from excessive chlorine use and tank inspection ladders were partially destroyed by corrosive chlorine in tank.

Additional information recorded included that air vents were not covered due to broken mesh on vents, inspection covers were highly corroded from excessive chlorine use and tank inspection ladders were partially destroyed by corrosive chlorine in tank.

Box 3.4 highlights that within the supply tanks simple maintenance tasks may be identified that will improve water quality in anticipation of the development of the WSP, including the repair of air vents, replacement of inspection hatches and the covering of outlet valves.

All available maps of the water distribution network should be examined. These maps will range from professional cartographic imagery to hand-drawn sketch maps. Where there are no existing maps, it is recommended that a detailed sketch map is done. Using expert judgment, the location of major infrastructure (water treatment works, service reservoirs, valve boxes, primary trunk mains) should be plotted. These do not need to be to scale and approximate distances of primary mains and secondary mains can be estimated on a reconnaissance field visit. The use of a Global Positioning System (GPS) device will greatly assist in the development of these maps as the plotting of locations and distances can be more accurately measured. Where a GPS is not available, it may still be possible to map locations accurately if reasonable maps exist and/or if there are suitable landmarks to fix locations using triangulation. Distances can be estimated in a number of ways; using reliable maps or surveying techniques.

Box A1.1 (see Annexe 1) outlines an example of how to gain a better understanding of a piped distribution system where **no** maps are available.

Once the map has been prepared, the key infrastructure points of the system should be identified in detail. This includes the service reservoirs, booster stations, transmission and trunk mains, secondary service mains and major valves. This book uses the following definitions:

- **Primary infrastructure** includes bulk transmission mains from the works to the service reservoirs, the service reservoirs themselves and the valves and other infrastructure on these that control flow.

- **Secondary service mains** are the principal supply pipes that deliver water from service reservoirs (or direct from the works) and to which community mains are connected. *Secondary infrastructure also includes any supply tanks, valves or other infrastructure that controls the flow of the system.*

Detailed flow diagrams should be prepared for the distribution system. Identifying how water flows through the system, major service reservoirs and the areas of distribution that each reservoir serve, major sluice valves, cross-connections between supply zones, major institutions, population densities, known leakage rates etc.

Zoning of supply

Zoning breaks the distribution system into manageable sections. The zoning process is outlined in Figure 3.2.

Zoning ensures that at any particular point in the supply staff know both the source of the water and the major infrastructure that the water has passed through. Furthermore, zoning of the system enables the operator to estimate the likely impact of a contaminant entering into the system at any given point. Each zone may be used to identify sanitary risks particular to individual sections of supply with the aim of improving the operators ability to manage overall risk.

The zones are defined by the hydraulics of the water distribution network. Where a computerized hydraulic model is available for the system, specific cut off valves

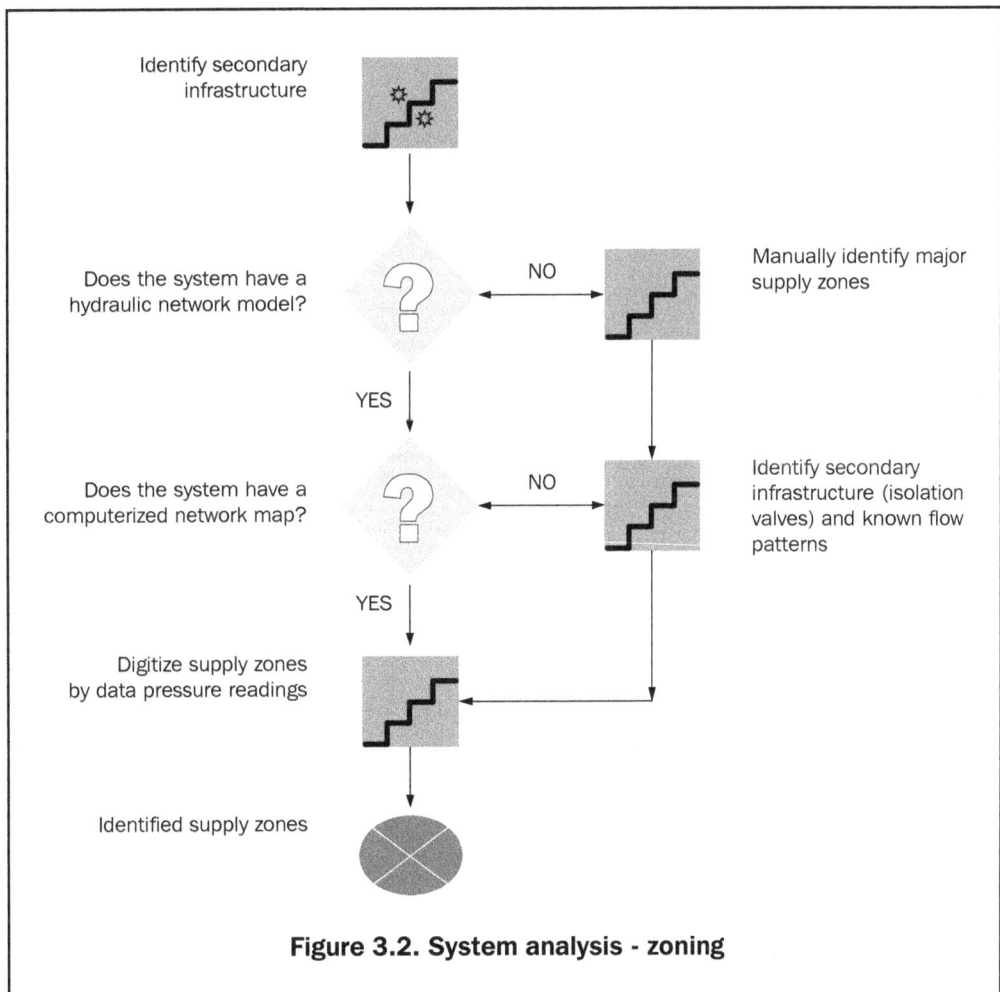

Figure 3.2. System analysis - zoning

(permanently closed valves) and hydraulic deviation zones are demarcated. These are identified by negative pressure readings in selected sections of the network. This process obviously requires data such as that outlined in Box A1.2 (see Annexe 1).

In the absence of extensive data or computerized models, expert judgement should be used to identify the existing closed valves in the system and the known flow paths within the network (see Box A1.3). Using the process outlined above, sketch maps of the system can be used and the operators of the system can mark on the maps the location of the permanently closed valves. Flow paths in the system can then be identified on the maps, showing the direction and extent of flow in the varied parts of the system.

An example of a sketch map approach can be seen in Box A1.3 (see Annexe 1). The drawing was done on site using A1 paper with the main infrastructure points being overlaid using tracing paper.

Identify intended uses and vulnerability

Following the zoning of the network, it is important to determine the intended use of water. This description may include:

- who the water is intended for and its intended use. What special considerations are in place for vulnerable groups such as infants, hospitalised patients, dialysis patients, the elderly and the immuno-compromized. Who the water is specifically not intended for;
- number of people served by different service levels (communal, yard, within-house);
- socio-economic status of different communities served;
- how water is to be used and what exposure routes are relevant;
- what consumer education is in place for water use and how this is communicated, including how consumers are notified of potential contamination.

This information is important as it will be used in the hazard analysis to determine the susceptibility of the consumer to contaminated water. Ample description of an intended use is provided in Box 3.5. This description provides the team with further understanding of the nature of the population served and any particular characteristics that may increase vulnerability to waterborne disease.

Box 3.5. Ample 'intended use' description

- NWSC in Kampala provides water to approximately half the population.

- The water is intended for general consumption by ingestion from drinking and food preparation. Dermal exposure also gained to waterborne hazards through washing of bodies and clothes.

- About half of the people served rely on water supplied from public taps, with a further significant proportion relying on tanker services filled from hydrants. The socio-economic level of the population served by public taps is low and vulnerability to poor health is consequently high. A significant proportion of the population is HIV positive, which increases vulnerability further.

Reviewing performance and environment data

The final desk-based stage in describing the system is to undertake an evaluation of existing data to assess the performance of the system. This will include reviewing water quality data to assess whether there are:

- areas where free chlorine residuals are lost;
- areas where turbidity is often raised;
- areas where microbial contamination has often been detected;
- areas where leakage is commonly reported; and
- areas of regular intermittence.

There may be a number of data sources to support this exercise, some from the water supplier and some from surveillance bodies. The purpose of collecting this data is to evaluate whether there are areas within the distribution system that might impact on water safety. Some of the data may be qualitative, for instance when doing this exercise in Kampala, the leakage data used was collected during community interviews as part of sanitary inspection because there was little existing quantitative leakage data. The data for intermittence was collected in a similar manner. It is preferable to use quantitative rather than qualitative data where possible.

Describing the environment around the system

It is important in developing the description of the distribution system to understand the environment around it and to consider what hazards or hazard sources it may contain that could affect the supply.

The data to collect includes:

- sanitation coverage data (on-site and off-site);
- location of sewers;
- location of drains;
- major roads;
- population data;
- population served by the supply by area;
- areas of industrial development;
- areas that are low lying.

Much of this data is collected as surrogates for hazard information. For instance, population density can be used as a surrogate for faecal loading (Howard, 2003). Others are more directly related to potential hazard events, for instance, sewers that are very close to water supply mains could lead to contamination events. This data will be used to identify priority areas for inspection during the field assessment stage and later incorporated into maps of hazardous events and risk.

Collecting data on the population served is very important for the later stage of risk ranking. To do this, information on the number of people that may be affected by a contamination event must be estimated, and this requires knowledge of how many people use the water downstream of the point of entry of a hazard.

Some data about the environment will be in a similar form to the water supply data and may be very easy to locate on the water supply map. This includes information such as the locations of sewers, roads and drains. Other data may be of a different nature and be less precisely related to the water supply systems. Examples include population density, population served, industrial development and sanitation coverage. All this data can be expressed in a less detailed manner than the water supply data and therefore these maps will show 'areas' of particular concern overlying the supply main rather than specific points.

Summary

At the end of Stage 2: System description and analysis, the team will have a set of maps that show:

- the supply's primary and secondary infrastructure;
- how many people use the water supply in different parts of the system;
- major hydraulic zones within the distribution system and thus water flows around the system;

- areas where there is evidence of failures in water quality/safety management as a means of identifying particular areas of concern;
- the environment within which the supply is found as a means of identifying potential hazardous areas;
- known water quality failures within zones of the network.

Chapter 4

Stage 3: Tools development and pilot activities

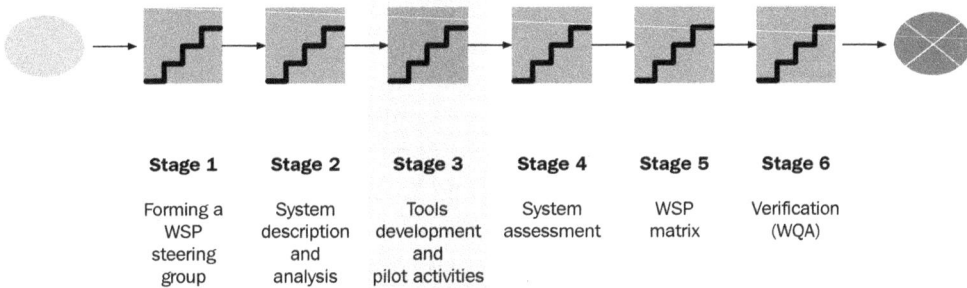

Stage 1	Stage 2	Stage 3	Stage 4	Stage 5	Stage 6
Forming a WSP steering group	System description and analysis	Tools development and pilot activities	System assessment	WSP matrix	Verification (WQA)

The next stage is to collect data from the field on the nature of the system, to investigate what risks exist that may affect the system, and to develop an understanding of how hazards could enter the supply and how these could be controlled. The first step in this process is to develop and pilot data collection tools. The tools used in a field assessment should be system specific and include sanitary inspections and the testing of selected physico-chemical parameters.

Before undertaking the assessment, consider your sanitary inspection tools. Findings from sanitary inspection field testing in the development of these guidelines noted the importance of standardization in order to maintain comparability. To achieve standardization, forms must be developed with personnel who have local knowledge of the design of individual facilities within the network (such as valve boxes, service reservoirs). These forms may be slightly different from the sanitary inspection forms used for monitoring, which may be modified for individual service reservoirs or valves.

It is recommended that two types of Sanitary Inspection (SI) tools are developed in order to assess and monitor sanitary risks within the system. These include:

- *Assessment tools* – A set of detailed quantitative tools designed to be used infrequently to assess the sanitary integrity of the system. These tools include water treatment plant audit forms and distribution system sanitary inspection forms.
- *Monitoring tools* – A set of tools designed to be used on a regular basis to monitor the sanitary integrity of specific points within the system. These tools include sanitary inspection forms specific to individual control points that provide information on the variable vulnerability within the supply.

Figure 4.1 outlines the appropriate first steps in developing sanitary inspection forms.

It is important to make a list of all known sanitary risks (or hazardous events) within the piped network. The team should consider all potential risks affecting the water supply and list each as a question. This should address all parts of the water supply system. As the lists can become very unwieldy, it is usually better to split the system into discrete common parts and develop sanitary inspection forms for each of these. For instance, there are likely to be forms specifically for:

- service reservoirs;
- major valves; and
- tapstands.

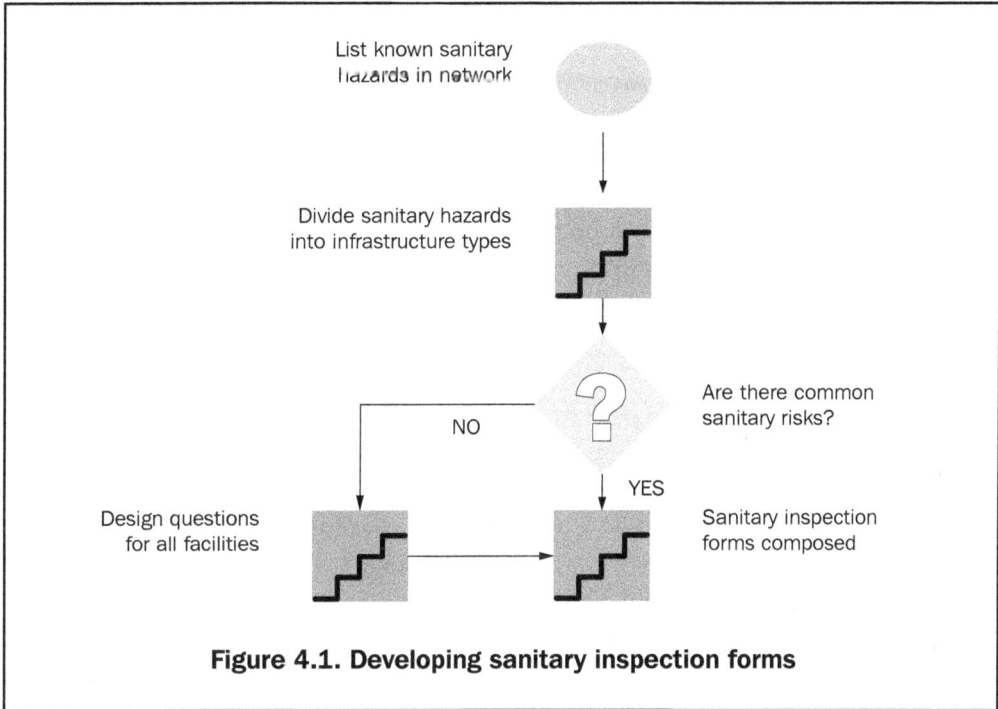

Figure 4.1. Developing sanitary inspection forms

It is often useful to start with forms used elsewhere to help develop the system-specific forms, but these should always be evaluated in relation to the actual system. Annexe 2 provides one set of example forms. The forms should be developed so that for each risk a question is asked that can be answered Yes or No.

- *Yes* answers mean that a risk is present;
- *No* means there is no risk.

The number of questions is immaterial, but it is better if the form is not too short (under 5 questions) or too long (over 20 questions). If it is too short then consider combining these questions with another sanitary inspection form. If it is too long, considering breaking the form into more than one form.

In developing the form, the first step should be for the team to use the risk map developed in Stage 2 to make a series of visits to different parts of the distribution system. At each point, the team should assess what risks could be present and note down a full list of potential problems that may need to be addressed on the sanitary inspection form. These should be reviewed in a workshop and the group should reach a consensus about what problems should be included. The next step is to phrase questions around the problems noted so that they can be included in a standard sanitary inspection form.

When developing the forms remember to use:

- simple phrasing;
- local terminology.

The inspection form may include questions that must be answered through some form of consumer interview. For instance, in systems where intermittence is not planned, questions may need to be included to ask consumers whether there has been intermittence in supply. For all parts of the system, the questions on the inspection forms will address the environment close to the point of inspection and the state of the infrastructure.

It is important that the end-users of the forms are able to understand the forms and to collect the information required rapidly and easily. This means that the questions on the form must be phrased in a way that ensures anyone using the form can understand what is being asked and simply by looking at the infrastructure be able to decide whether the risk is present or absent. It is essential that the forms are field-tested by the team by visiting, completing the forms and analysing the results. The inspector should then assess whether they feel that they have gained the knowledge required. If not, the forms should be amended and re-tested until they are appropriate.

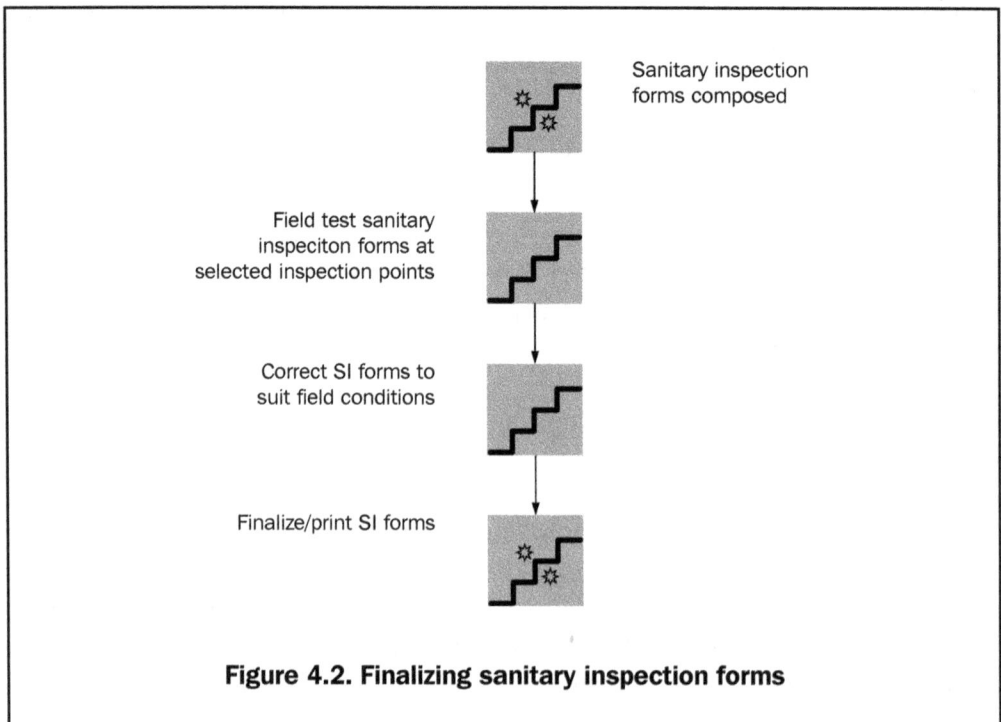

Figure 4.2. Finalizing sanitary inspection forms

Box 4.1. Development of sanitary inspection forms

Kampala is served by five different service reservoirs. In-depth field verification of potential sanitary risks in each service reservoir revealed individual engineering design differences between the service reservoirs. In order to maintain comparability, sanitary risks common to all the reservoirs were identified.

For example: Tress could damage both below ground, elevated service reservoirs and overhanging trees branches could provide a ready access route for bird droppings into elevated tanks and service reservoir; and tree roots could damage the reservoir walls, resulted in the phrasing of a question common to both designs:

Can trees have an impact on the reservoir?   Yes/No

(e.g. tree roots, overhanging branches, etc.)

Specific questions of SI form development are outlined in Box 4.1.

As well as the creation of SI forms, equipment to test physical-chemical parameters should be selected (see Figure 4.3).

It is recommended that (as a minimum) the following parameters should be tested:

- **Free residual chlorine** – to assess residual disinfectant protection available throughout piped network if chlorine disinfection is used. For the systems that use UV or ozonation, greater reliance should be placed on turbidity.
- **Total residual chlorine** – to assess whether loss of free chlorine is related to either a failure in chlorination or consumption from contaminants in the system. Again, this is only suitable for chlorinated supplies.
- **pH** – to assess whether chlorination had been performed within an acceptable range for effective chlorination (pH should be below 8).
- **Turbidity** – to assess whether there is likely to be increased chlorine consumption from either ingress, biofilm sloughing or disturbance of sediment.

To undertake the relevant analyses, it is recommended that field testing water quality equipment is used (e.g. hand-held chlorine/pH/conductivity/turbidity meter). Appropriate training in the use of this equipment should be undertaken as part of a field trial prior to undertaking the in-depth system assessment.

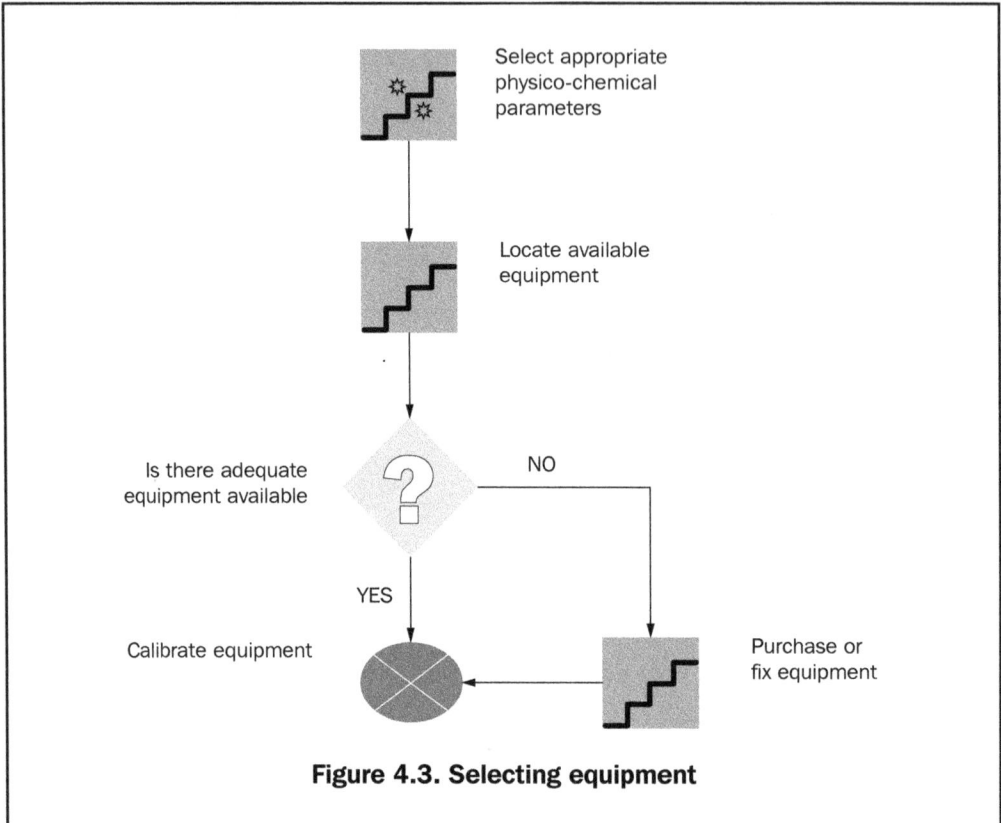

Figure 4.3. Selecting equipment

Summary

At the end of this stage, the team should be aware of the importance and be competent in:

- developing, trialling and finalizing Sanitary Inspection (SI) forms;
- selecting appropriate physico-chemical parameters; and
- operating appropriate field testing equipment.

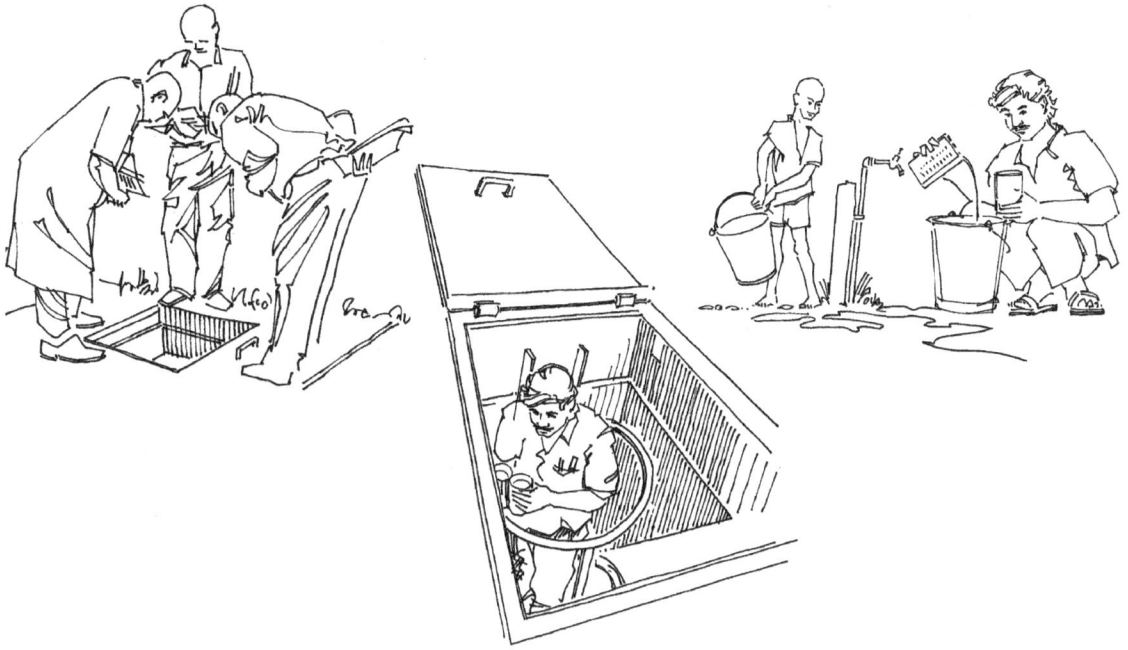

Chapter 5

Stage 4: System assessment

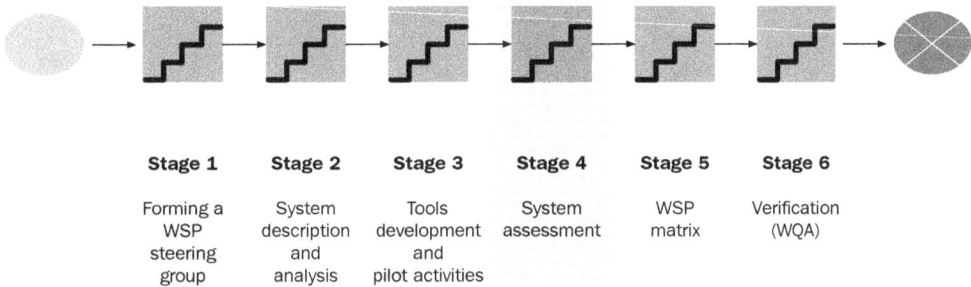

Stage 1	Stage 2	Stage 3	Stage 4	Stage 5	Stage 6
Forming a WSP steering group	System description and analysis	Tools development and pilot activities	System assessment	WSP matrix	Verification (WQA)

The objective of the system assessment is to verify the information gathered on the network from Stage 2. Using information gathered in the system description and analysis, inspection points within the network should then be identified for field inspection. As the WSP is an iterative process, information gathered during the system analysis will be used to select the inspection points that are assessed in the field during Stage 4. These are identified using the selection criteria outlined in Box 5.1.

Due to the complexity of water distribution systems, it is recommended that points are identified according to the hydraulic supply zones. The use of supply zones for identifying inspection points ensures that the system assessment can be divided into manageable sections and also ensures that the results can be used to check whether any large-scale problems are noted, as the results can be linked to areas served by single service reservoirs or treatment works. The zone in which each inspection point is located should be recorded.

All the service reservoirs and valves located on primary and secondary mains should be included in the assessment. For instance 46 valves on primary and secondary mains in the Kampala system were included in the initial assessment.

Box 5.1. Inspection point selection criteria

Hazardous environment	Proximity to physical hazard (sewer, low lying area)
	Proximity to area of high faecal loading (population density)
Evidence of previous problems	Historical record of microbial contamination
	Historical record of intermittence in supply
	Historical record of leakage
	Evidence of frequent low residual chlorine levels
System characteristics of vulnerability	Proximity to primary/secondary infrastructure
	Pipe attribute (age/material/length)
	Pressure/supply zone
	Proximity to identified part of the system considered very vulnerable(??)
Susceptibility	Number of people affected downstream

This was very useful because it highlighted not only a range of consistent problems with design and maintenance, but also that some of the valves were not accessible and would have to be excluded from future planned inspections. Where there are a large number of valves, a sample of those on secondary mains may be selected for regular inspection taking into account the issues outlined further below.

In addition to primary and secondary infrastructure, a sample of points within the tertiary infrastructure should also be visited. This provides an opportunity to assess on the ground what types of risks may affect water safety close to consumer taps, and to also assess whether the major risks to water safety lie at a very local level or within the major infrastructure.

In selecting a sample of secondary and tertiary inspection points, it is important to use the data collated during the system description and analysis stage regarding the environment within which the mains are found. In the assessment, it is important to select sites that represent the range of selected criteria. When considering the factors noted in Box 5.1, sample sites should be selected with or without those factors. This helps to determine how important such factors are in creating problems.

A key part of the site selection is to consider the characteristics of the system as a means of identifying areas of different vulnerability to contamination. These characteristics are also used to develop risk maps which help select the critical points identified during the system analysis that need further assessment in the field. There are three methods that can be used to develop risk maps:

1. *Qualitative risk assessments* – In the absence of a GIS database, these methods enable operators to assess and manage risk in their network.
2. *Semi-Quantitative risk assessment* – This method involves the computation of variable risk levels based on semi-quantitative ranking methods into a GIS database.
3. *Modelling-based assessments* – The use of composite programming to estimate risk weightings for individual variables.

The third of these methods is discussed in the accompanying documents in this guidelines series. To support the development of a WSP, methods 1 and 2 are very appropriate and are designed to provide detail on the static or inherent risk associated with the system. Common to each of these approaches is the identification of indicators. These include the identification of pipe attributes and the hazardous environment in which pipes are found. The combination of these variables into a risk matrix forms the basis for the development of risk maps.

The development of risk maps assists the WSP as it aids the identification of points of risk within the supply and prioritises areas to control water safety within the system. As pipe networks are underground, risk maps assist the WSP steering team to assess and manage surrogate measures of risk within the distribution system. These surrogates may include vulnerability assessments based on pipe material or hazard assessments using population density as a surrogate of faecal loading. The use of these surrogates helps prioritise which of the pipes is at greatest risk of contamination.

However, levels of information on both hazard and vulnerability in supply will vary according to the extent of data records. This information can be obtained from a number of sources including:

- review of supply records;
- review of maintenance records;
- sanitary inspection data.

It can equally be obtained from an understanding of the relationship between the pipe attributes (material, diameter, age) and the environment in which it is laid.

Once risk estimates have been established for the above indicators, it is recommended that an overall risk score is assigned to each inspection point within the supply. Using the quantitative risk estimate approach, it is possible to combine all the sub variables to calculate a total risk score. This may follow the example outlined in Box 5.2.

It is also important to select a range of inspection points from different hazardous environments in order to gain a representative overview of the system. Previous water quality data may also be used to ensure that inspections are carried out in areas of known previous problems and areas that have been relatively free of problems. This process is summarized in Figure 5.1. At each point visited, a reading should be taken to fix the point precisely. This is most effective when using GPS but triangulation can also be used where there are reliable maps and available landmarks or at the very least a sketchmap.

Box 5.2. Risk ranking table

			Namirembe booster	Namirembe parish	Pipe number 2209
		STATIC VULNERABILITY		M	
VULNERABILITY	Performance monitoring data	Leakage (p/a)		H	
		Discontinuity (p/a)		M	
		Pipe breakage (p/a)		L	
	Pipe attributes	RISK		M	
		Age			
		RISK		H	
		Material		ST	
		RISK		M	
		Diameter (mm)			100
		RISK		M	
		Length (m)			474
HAZARD	Hazard environment	RISK		L	
		Low lying area		N	
	Hazard source	RISK		L	
		Parish (POP)		Namirembe	
SUSCEPTIBILITY		RISK		H	
		Roof type		H	
		House type		VL	
		Sampling point category		Booster station	
		Sampling point	Namirembe booster	Namirembe parish	Pipe number 2209

Key
p/a = per annum, VL = Very Low, L = Low, M = Medium, H = High

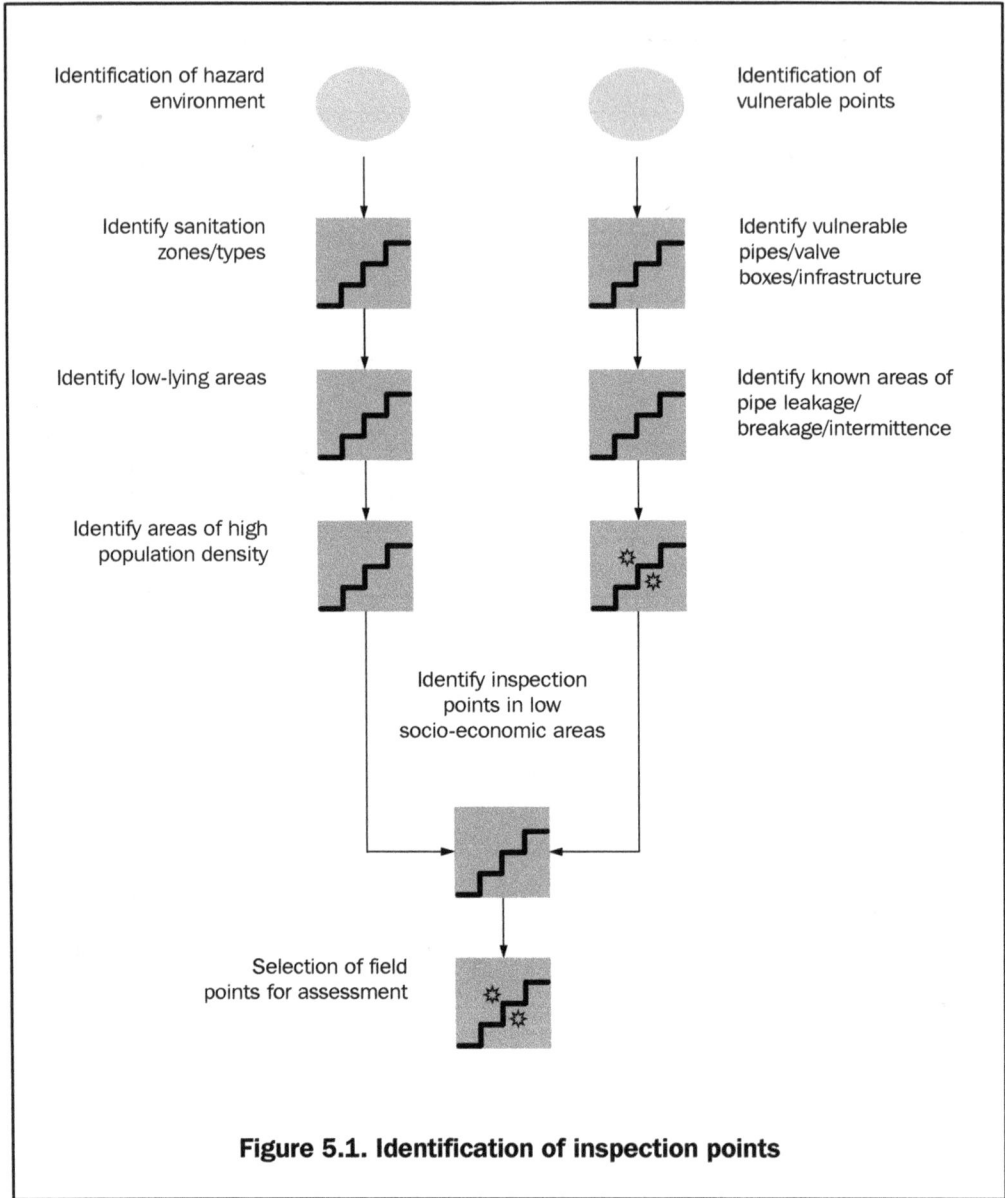

Figure 5.1. Identification of inspection points

An example of inspection point selection is outlined in Box 5.3.

Once the inspection points have been identified they are listed according to the sub zone in which they are located. If block maps exist for the system, these can be used to assist in the identification of the points.

Box 5.3. Selecting inspection points in Guntur, India

During the system analysis stage of the development of the WSP, the steering group identified a total of 206 risk points within the supply. The next step was to select the highest risk points as they would require assessment in the field. Of the total 206 points, inaccessible points such as buried valves boxes were discounted and then the data from the following sources was used to select the points:

- Hazard and vulnerability – findings from Stage 2: System analysis and system description
- Institutional knowledge – known points of vulnerability within the system
- Susceptibility – data from the field survey and the team's knowledge of the Guntur socio economic zones.

In total **163** points were selected for the Guntur supply. Initially these included all the primary infrastructure such as service reservoirs along with booster pumps/tanks and principle secondary infrastructure. Using historical records of leakage and chlorine residual data, an equal spread of points within the supply was chosen.

Practical considerations in the field assessment

It is essential that the assessment is properly planned and that the type of data collected be considered before the assessment is implemented. Once the sample sites have been selected they should be marked on the map and an estimate made of how many sites could be visited in one day. Hence, the total number of days required can then be calculated. Route maps for each day's fieldwork should be prepared in advance and discussed with the inspectors covering that area. It is more cost-effective to visit several different sites yeilding different types of data in one area per day than to only visit points of a particular type in different areas. Thus the assessment teams should move through the system in a progressive manner. It is essential that staff have forms for all the different types of inspection points within each area, as well as daily record sheets for water quality data recording. The process for planning and implementing assessments is shown in the flow chart in Figure 5.2.

Summary

At the end of this stage the team will have a good understanding of how to undertake a system assessment. This includes:
- identifying inspection points;
- inspect point criteria;
- undertake a field assessment;
- tools and equipment required for field assessment.

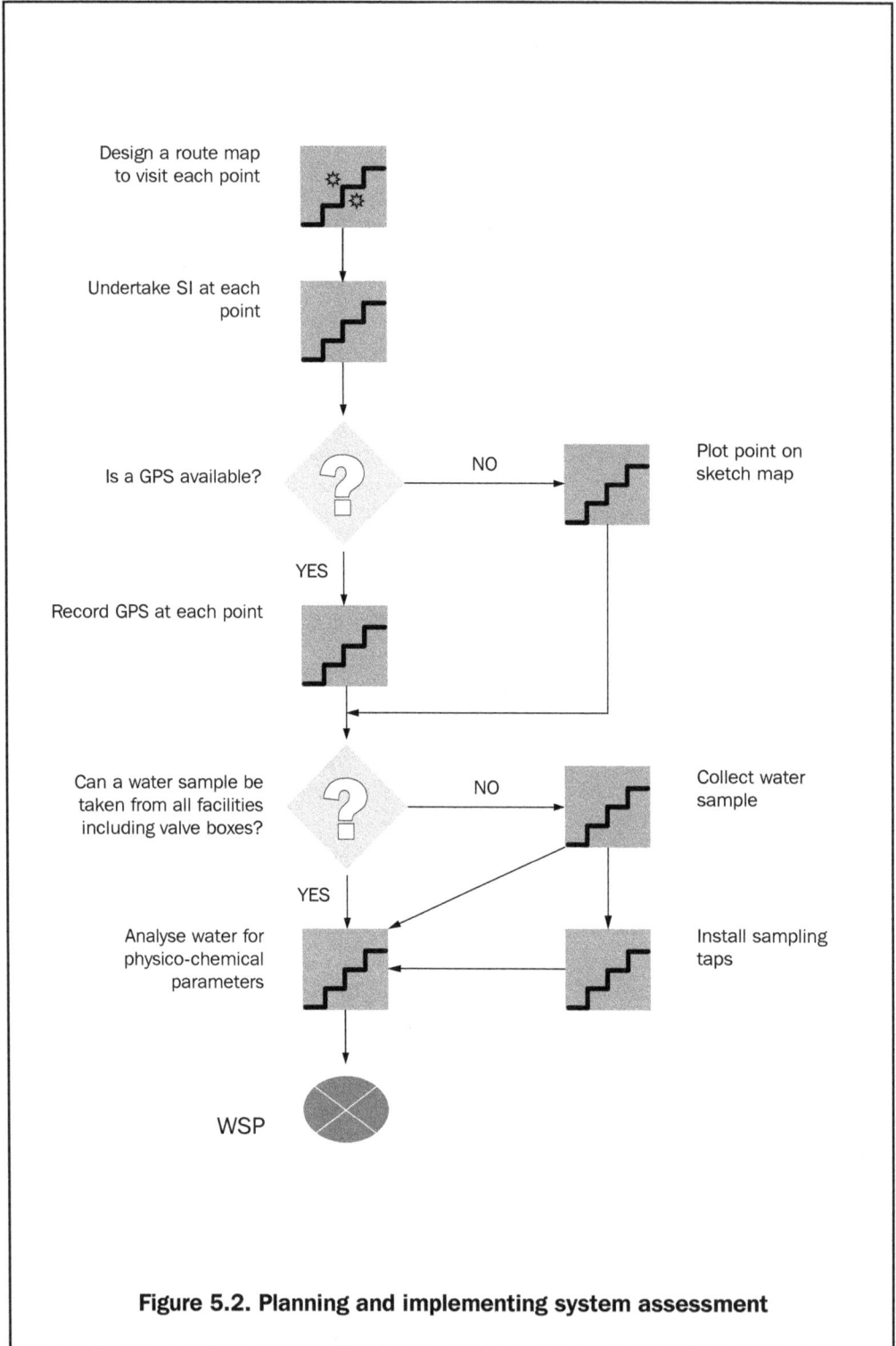

Figure 5.2. Planning and implementing system assessment

Chapter 6

Stage 5: Developing the WSP

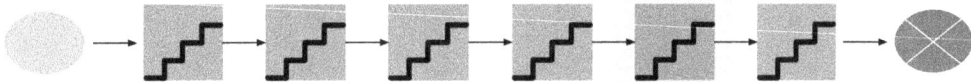

Stage 1	Stage 2	Stage 3	Stage 4	Stage 5	Stage 6
Forming a WSP steering group	System description and analysis	Tools development and pilot activities	System assessment	WSP matrix	Verification (WQA)

Once the data on the system and hazards has been collected, the draft WSP can be developed. The WSP progresses through a number of key stages as shown in Figure 6.1 and is developed for each type of infrastructure within the supply. For example, a Water Safety Plan managing matrix would be developed for each of the water treatment works, service reservoir, valves, supply tanks, etc. As each of these points of supply has varying levels of risk, it is recommended that results from the system assessment are used to define specific sanitary risks for each of

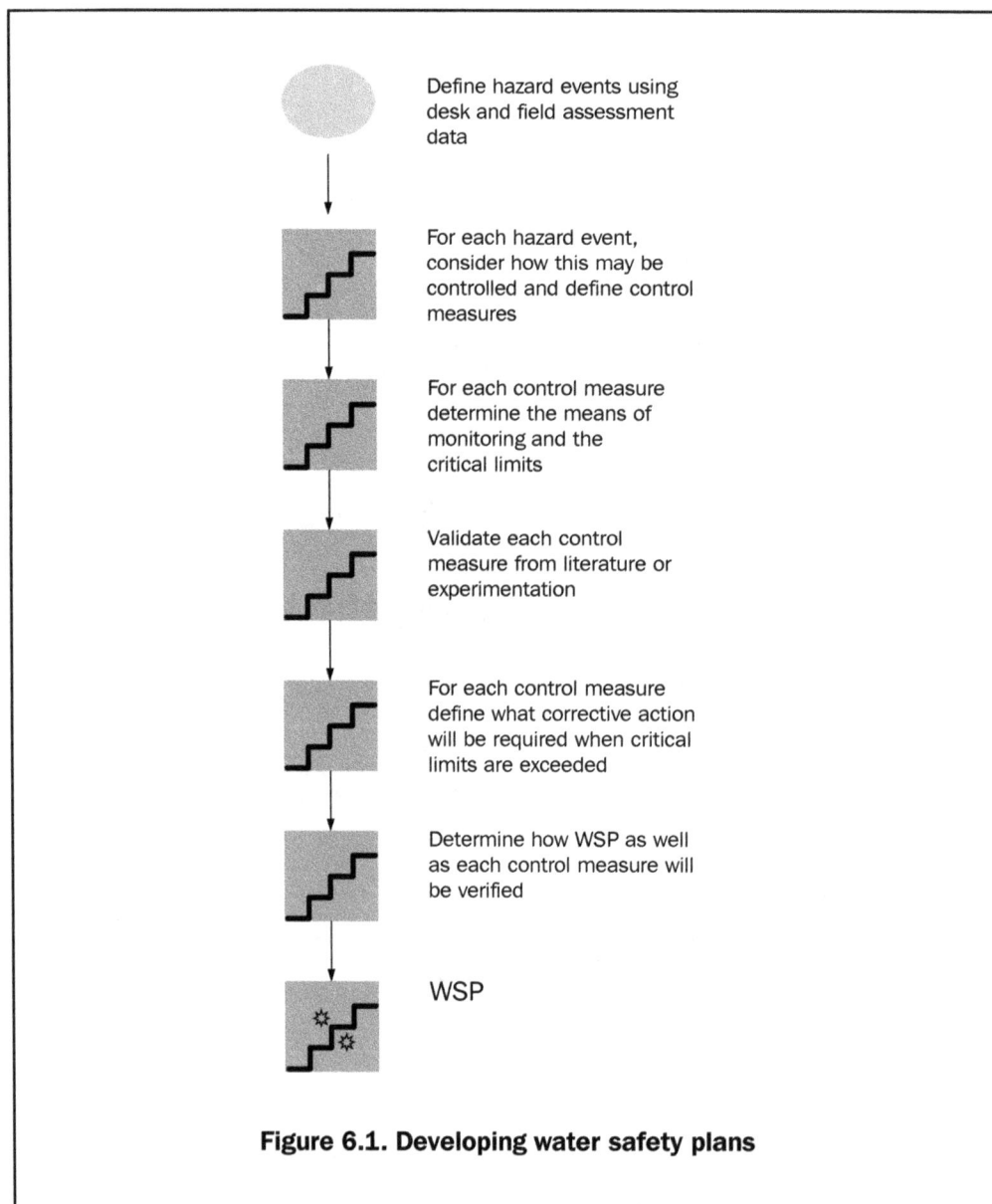

Define hazard events using desk and field assessment data

For each hazard event, consider how this may be controlled and define control measures

For each control measure determine the means of monitoring and the critical limits

Validate each control measure from literature or experimentation

For each control measure define what corrective action will be required when critical limits are exceeded

Determine how WSP as well as each control measure will be verified

WSP

Figure 6.1. Developing water safety plans

the identified inspection points within the supply. This can be done following the flow diagram in Figure 6.1.

Hazard events

This section provides guidance on how to develop the WSP matrix. It begins with examples and definitions of hazard events and continues by describing each stage of the WSP matrix through to the corrective action. At each stage of the matrix an example is provided.

Hazard event is?

Hazard event	Cause	Risk	Control measure	Critical limits		Monitoring			Corrective action
				Target	Action	What	When	Who	
Microbial contamination of service reservoir from birds									

The first step in considering hazards which may affect the water supply is to identify potential hazards during the desk-based system assessment and the subsequent field assessment. This should identify both the type of specific hazard (e.g. chemicals, bacteria, viruses, protozoa) and the sources of hazards (e.g. sewers, on-site sanitation, drains, industries, etc).

In developing the WSP, the next step is to consider the impact of these hazards on the water supply. Experience has shown that in developing WSPs considering 'hazard events' rather than specific hazards is the most effective way to identify and quantify risks to water safety (Deere, 2001). A hazard event in this context can be defined as a mechanism by which a contaminant of health concern is introduced into the water supply.

In water treatment works hazard events tend to be related to specific failures in treatment processes, for instance breakthrough of protozoa because of short-

---

Box 6.1. Source – Pathway – Receptor relationship

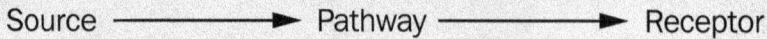

Source ⟶ Pathway ⟶ Receptor

Source – Hazard event/environment
Pathway – Vulnerability of piped supply
Receptor – Receiving water infrastructure

---

circuiting of settlers or breakthrough of bacteria caused by a failure in disinfection. For treatment processes, therefore, it is essential to develop hazard events that relate to problems that can or have been encountered in the operation of that particular type of treatment works.

In order to identify a hazard event in distribution systems, it is important to consider the source-pathway-receptor model of contamination, which is shown in Box 6.1. In this model the source is the source of the hazards, the receptor is the water supply (in this case the pipes that form the distribution system) and pathways are the means by which the hazards can leave the 'source' and reach the 'receptor'.

The source-pathway-receptor model recognises that the presence of a hazard in the environment is insufficient on its own to represent a risk; a feasible pathway must exist that allow hazards to travel from the source to the water supply. When this occurs, it is a 'hazard event'. In developing the WSP from the data collected during desk and field assessments, it is important to consider whether it is feasible for the hazard to leave its source, travel through the soil and enter the water pipe. For instance, drinking-water mains pipes are often laid deeper than sewer pipes and therefore it would be expected that a reasonable pathway (and so hazard event) exists if the mains pipes pass through soil, that has become saturated from a leaking sewer.

When considering hazard events, be aware that there may be some hazard events for which controls are already in place. An example is the presence of a cut-off wall between a sewer and mains pipe. The hazard event of sewage-contaminated water entering the mains pipe is still valid, but the team will need to consider how they wish to conceptualise the hazard event. For instance, the hazard event could be 'cut-off wall fails allowing sewage-contaminated water to submerge the mains pipe.'

Alternatively, the hazard event could be 'sewage contaminated water submerges mains pipe'. Either way of presentation is valid and the control measure may not in fact change significantly. It is, however, important for the understanding of the system and in determining whether the control measure is in place or whether the supplier needs to invest in a new control measure.

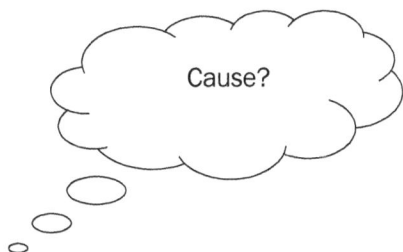

Hazard event	Cause	Risk	Control measure	Critical limits		Monitoring			Corrective action
				Target	Action	What	When	Who	
Microbial contamination of service reservoir from birds	Birds' faeces enter through open inspection hatches								

Once it is accepted that a hazard may reach the mains pipe, a hazard event describing the process should be defined. An example is shown in Box 6.2.

Box 6.2. Hazard event scenario

Hazard Source = Sewer, drain, bird roosting on service reservoir

Hazard Movement Release = Leaking sewer, infiltration from drain, defecating bird

Hazard Pathway = Effluent from sewer, grey water flush in drains, rain washing bird faeces

Hazard Receptor = Pipe leaks (i.e. has holes), pipe is submerged

= HAZARD EVENT

It is also important to identify where in the system the event could occur. This is important for the risk ranking stage, identifying priorities and developing operational monitoring plans. Defining hazard events where they could not really occur wastes resources and results in poorly directed WSPs. For instance, cross-contamination between a sewer and a water main cannot occur in non-sewered areas. Equally, contamination of service reservoir by bird faeces resulting from an inspection cover being left open can only occur at a service reservoir that has an inspection cover.

Locating where the hazard event could occur in the system is important in the risk ranking approach. In this approach, the relative risk of the hazard event is determined in the following way:

1. Consider the likelihood of occurrence and the severity of the impact which should be done through a qualitative or semi-quantitative approach.
2. Consider the likelihood of an event occurring - it is important to remember that all events can happen. For instance, the risk of bird faeces entering an open inspection cover at a service reservoir is likely to occur. Service reservoirs are inspected often and it is likely that an inspection cover be left open regularly. Equally birds are likely to perch on the top of a service reservoir and are likely to defecate.
3. Consider prioritizing the occurrence of events - for instance, the risk of ingress of contaminated water into mains pipes may be more likely to occur in older parts of the system, in parts of the system with ductile iron pipes than in newer parts of the system with uPVC pipes. Developing this level of detailed understanding of the system and the hazard events that occur is important in estimating the risks of events occurring and prioritizing areas for control.

Severity

Severity is usually gauged in relation to both the number of people affected and the likely impact on those affected (for instance separated into morbidity and mortality). The nature of the hazards will determine the likely health outcome (for instance pathogens and massive pollution by chemicals may lead to mortality, whereas lower levels of chemicals may only lead to morbidity).

When estimating severity and defining severity profiles, it is important for the WSP team to consider the impact of short-term and long-term exposures. This may result in some long-term chemical exposures (e.g. to arsenic from source water) being given a higher severity rating than short-term exposures alone.

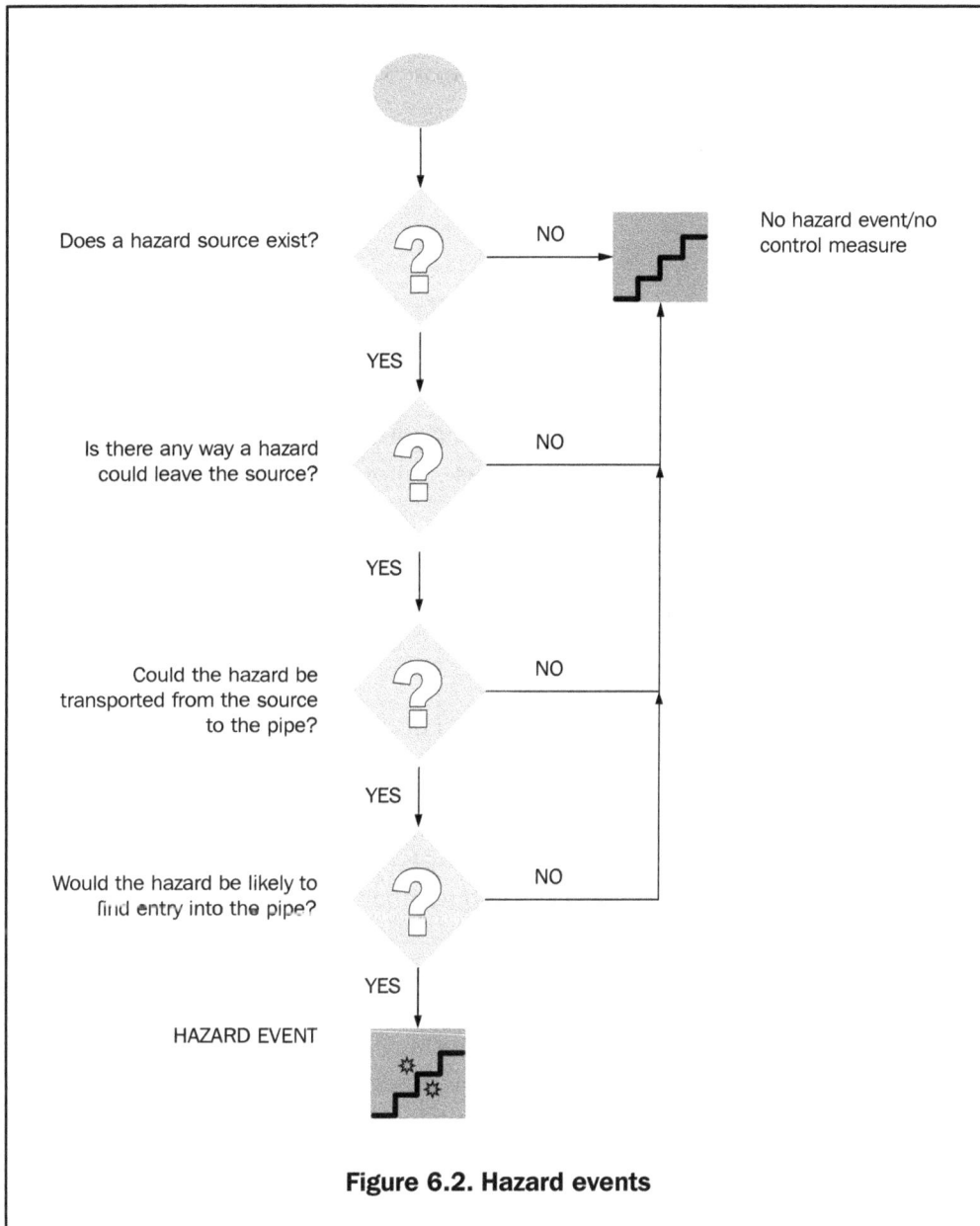

Figure 6.2. Hazard events

The location of the hazard event will influence the number of people affected, for instance hazard events on major transmission mains or in service reservoirs will be likely to have an impact on many people, whereas a hazard event in a small tertiary pipe may only affect a very small number of people. This approach can be further refined by considering the vulnerability or susceptibility of the users affected and whether this will influence the outcome. For instance, poorer communities will be more susceptible to many waterborne pathogens and therefore hazard events that affect these groups may have a greater severity than those that affect higher income groups.

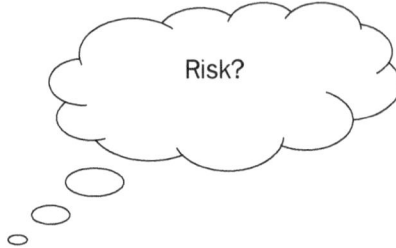

Risk?

Hazard event	Cause	Risk	Control measure	Critical limits		Monitoring			Corrective action
				Target	Action	What	When	Who	
Microbial contamination of service reservoir from birds	Birds' faeces enter through open inspection hatches	Moderate/ catastrophic							

A risk-ranking matrix should be developed to address both likelihood and severity. Most approaches use some form of semi-quantitative ranking system by allocating numbers to different levels of likelihood and different levels of severity. A risk score is then calculated by multiplying these two numbers together as shown below.

Risk = Likelihood x Severity

The selection of the categories and the weighting allocated to different categories should be considered by the WSP team, as at present there is no uniform 'industry standard'. Guidelines to definitions are provided in Box 6.3. It should be noted that semi-quantitative estimates are sufficient at this level.

The weightings used in Box 6.2 were applied in South-East Water, Australia (Deere et al., 2001) and in Uganda (Godfrey et al., 2002). These are applied to each of the inspection points in order to define the severity of risk associated with individual hazard events in piped supply.

The purpose of the table is to provide the users with a means by which to prioritise the risks to be controlled. In using these approaches, it is also important to use common sense. After categorizing hazard events, review them to make sure that

Box 6.3. Risk and severity, some guidelines to definitions – *Deere et al., 2001*

Likelihood	Definition
Almost certain	Once a day
Likely	Once per week
Moderate	Once per month
Unlikely	Once per year
Rare	Once every 5 years
Impact	**Definition**
Catastrophic	Potentially lethal to large population
Major	Potentially lethal to small population
Moderate	Potentially harmful to large population
Minor	Potentially harmful to small population
Insignificant	No impact or not detectable

they make sense. For instance, make sure priority is not given to events that happen often but have little effect over rare events that kill people! This may require the team to revisit some of the decisions made and re-evaluate the category of severity or likelihood ascribed.

Determining control measures

For each hazard event, a control measure must be determined with associated critical limits that describe whether the control measure is functioning correctly (in compliance) or control is being lost (out of compliance). Control measures must be actions that can be taken that will prevent the hazard event from occurring and it should be clear from the description of the control measure what will be done to reduce the risks. The control measure is therefore closely related to how the hazard event was presented. Using the example of how we could present a hazard event relating to a mains pipe submerged in sewage leaking from a sewer, the control measure could be 'a cut-off wall of X depth be maintained between the drinking supply main and the sewer'.

Control measures may already be in place and therefore the WSP will simply be a way to document/record how safety is already assured and to emphasise the importance of these measures. In other cases, the control measure may be a new working practice that must be introduced and therefore the WSP will justify why the new practice is required.

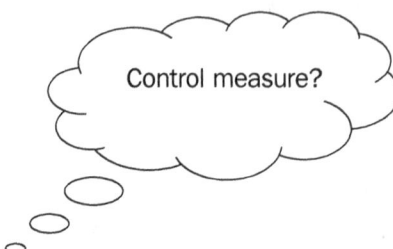

Control measure?

Hazard event	Cause	Risk	Control measure	Critical limits		Monitoring			Corrective action
				Target	Action	What	When	Who	
Microbial contamination of service reservoir from birds	Birds' faeces enter through open inspection hatches	Moderate/ catastrophic	Inspection covers remain in place						

In some other cases, the control measure will require investment. These investments cannot be included in the operational WSP, but must be identified and included in a list of needs for water safety management. In these cases, the utility should identify how this investment will be secured and planned. In the meantime, the immediate action may be limited to ongoing monitoring of water safety problems resulting from a lack of control measures.

In identifying the control measure, the team should consider the nature of the hazard event, the hazard source, the entry point into the supply and where intervention will be most cost-effectively applied. Control of a hazard event can be achieved through actions:

- at the hazard source (removal, containment or treatment);
- that break the pathway (removal, containment or diversion);
- at the supply (prevention of entry or treatment).

It will always be preferred that action is taken at the hazard source or pathway rather than at the supply, as these are 'upstream' actions. By preference control will also focus on removal or at least containment of hazards and pathways, such as the example in Box 6.4, rather than treatment of either the hazard or the supply, as these are preventive actions.

Box 6.4. Removing hazards – lessons from the UK

A utility water supply in the UK noted a problem with Cryptosporidium in its source waters during periods of lambing. In response, they initiated an activity to remove pregnant ewes from the catchment each year and have found a very significant reduction in Cryptosporidium presence in their water.

The selection of the appropriate control measure will be influenced by the feasibility of the actions and the relative cost; thus, whilst it would be preferable to remove hazard sources or their pathways, it may actually be more cost-effective to focus on the water supply. In some cases, intervention at hazard sources may not be possible immediately as actions may be required by other organizations or will take time to implement. Actions at both hazard sources and on pathways may still leave residual hazards within the environment which may require additional controls; therefore, it is likely that for many hazard events some control measure will be required at the water supply itself to prevent ingress into the supply. Actions will often be required at the hazard source, to break the pathway, and at the water supply

Box 6.5. Control measure examples

Action	Examples
Removal of hazard source	Removal of animals from catchment at key times Removal of on-site sanitation from recharge area
Containment of the hazard source	Pit latrine designs Concrete lining on drains Lining landfills Impervious oil storage Chemical waste Reduced sewer leakage
Treatment at the hazard source	Leachate treatment at landfill sites Wastewater treatment Industrial waste treatment
Breaking pathways	Cut-off walls between sewers and water supply mains Protected vents at service reservoirs
Preventing pre-cursors	Fencing at service reservoirs Reducing traffic loads on mains pipes
Action at the supply	Reduced leakage (less ingress) Reduced intermittence
Minor	Potentially harmful to small population
Insignificant	No impact or not detectable

in order to secure sustained water safety. In some cases, the control measure may focus on a 'pre-cursor' to a hazard event. For example, an aspect whose presence or absence will make it easier for the hazard event to occur. The lack of a fence for instance, increases the likelihood of a number of hazard events (such as direct ingress of animals faeces through damaged pipes and access by animals to service reservoirs), but a fence itself would not result in a hazard event (see Box 6.5 for control measure examples).

Setting critical limits

For each control measure, critical limits must be established that will provide the basis of a judgement as to whether the control measure is out of compliance and therefore action is required.

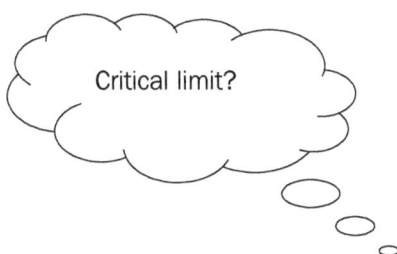

Critical limit?

Hazard event	Cause	Risk	Control measure	Critical limits		Monitoring			Corrective action
				Target	Action	What	When	Who	
Microbial contamination of service reservoir from birds	Birds' faeces enter through open inspection hatches	Moderate/ catastrophic	Inspection covers remain in place	Inspection covers locked in place	Inspection covers not in place or locked				

The nature of critical limits will vary, but there can be a lower limit (e.g. a minimum concentration of residual free chlorine), an upper limit (for instance a high sanitary risk score observed through sanitary inspection) or an envelope of performance (for instance pH within a specified range for effective chlorination). Although critical limits are by definition levels of performance at which action must be taken to ensure that control is maintained, they should be set at a level where exceeding the limits will not result in a significant risk to health. Critical limits must be directly or indirectly measurable or observable: otherwise, control performance cannot be assessed. Box 6.6 provides some examples of critical limits for a variety of control points.

Box 6.6. Critical limits for a variety of control points

Control point	Critical limit	
	Target	Action
Treatment works (Gravity flow rapid sand filters)	90% reduction in turbidity	Turbidity of <5NTU
Service reservoirs	Inspection covers locked in place	Inspection covers missing
Valve box	Packing not leaking	Evidence of leaking valves

Defining a critical limit depends on exactly how the control measure exerts control over hazards or hazard events. Where the control measure involves some element of control over hazard sources (for instance the proximity of pit latrines to a borehole) then the critical limit will be the absence of the hazard source or its presence will be limited to a prescribed density. In some cases, the critical limit may be related to a factor that controls the development of a pathway, for example, fencing around a groundwater abstraction point would prevent animals from damaging the headworks or defecating close to the wellhead.

In many cases, controls are established in relation to treatment processes such as chlorination, and in these situations the critical limits will be dictated by the point at which the effective removal of hazards from the water no longer occurs, for instance, less than 0.1mg/l of free chlorine residual in a distribution system.

Validation

Each control measure and critical limit should be validated to ensure that the proposed control measures will be able to control the identified hazard to an acceptable level and that the critical limits are accurate in terms of potential breakthrough. Validation may be done either on the supply itself using natural organisms, or non-toxic index organisms and tracers through challenge experiments in laboratories.

In many cases, the same organisms used for verification will also be deployed in validation. However, when undertaking validation an essential component is to assess the likely health risk that may be derived from the lack of control. This can take the form of a risk assessment; the results of which will determine whether additional control measures are needed. The use of quantitative microbial and chemical risk assessments are recommended for such risk assessments. This is not described in detailed in the accompanying documents in this series.

Monitoring

Every control measure needs a system to monitor its performance in relation to the critical limits. Monitoring should concentrate on parameters directly related to process control and should use methods that provide results that can be easily interpreted at the time of measurement or observation

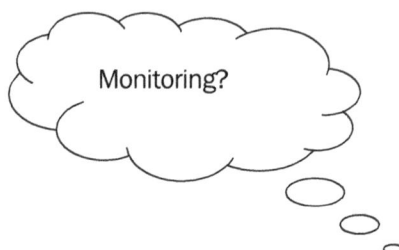

Monitoring?

Hazard event	Cause	Risk	Control measure	Critical limits		Monitoring			Corrective action
				Target	Action	What	When	Who	
Microbial contamination of service reservoir from birds	Birds' faeces enter through open inspection hatches	Moderate/ catastrophic	Inspection covers remain in place	Inspection covers locked in place	Inspection covers not in place or locked	Sanitary inspection Chlorine residual	Daily	Operating staff	

The frequency of monitoring for control points depends to a large extent on the nature of the control measure, the critical limits and the rapidity with which change may be expected to occur. The performance of some control measures can be expected to vary widely and change rapidly, and require frequent (and sometimes online) monitoring. This will typically include most control measures on treatment processes (e.g. chlorine dosing, coagulant dosing, filtration). In other cases, monitoring may be carried out frequently, but not online, for instance daily inspection of infrastructure or service reservoir covers. In other cases the monitoring may be very infrequent, for instance the number of animals in the catchment is a control measure so monitoring may be restricted to annual or six-monthly checks.

Corrective actions

For each control measure identified, the team should outline a corrective measure that will be undertaken to prevent contaminated water being supplied, if, monitoring demonstrates that the critical limit has been exceeded. Although it may not be possible to define all actions required in advance, it is important to define some course of action to follow. This is important as part of an overall preventive management approach. If a control measure is identified where no corrective action is needed, then it is essential that the water supplier undertakes further work to identify what options exist to rectify non-compliance.

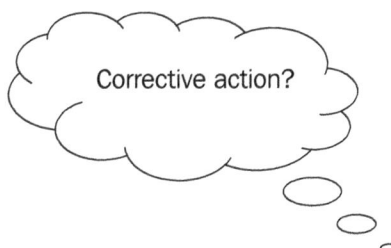

Corrective action?

Hazard event	Cause	Risk	Control measure	Critical limits		Monitoring			Corrective action
				Target	Action	What	When	Who	
Microbial contamination of service reservoir from birds	Birds' faeces enter through open inspection hatches	Moderate/ catastrophic	Inspection covers remain in place	Inspection covers locked in place	Inspection covers not in place or locked	Sanitary inspection Chlorine residual	Daily	Operating staff	Replace inspection cover and check chlorine consumption

The nature of corrective action depends on the nature of the control measure. Corrective action may consist of several interventions: immediate action to prevent the supply of unsafe drinking-water (switching to an alternative source, emergency chlorination, advising consumers to boil water before drinking etc); and bringing the control measure back into compliance. If actions do not have an impact on either of these stages, they should not be considered as corrective actions. Figure 6.3 illustrates the decision-making process to identify a corrective action.

Corrective actions may require regular revision and there should be a regular review of working practices, best practice guidelines and available literature to ensure that the corrective actions are those most appropriate and effective. When incidents occur within the system, it is essential that the corrective actions proposed are: reviewed to assess their efficacy; assessed to see whether they should be included as a corrective action; and assessed to determine whether any other actions are required for the future.

In a few cases the severity of a hazard event may not be known and in these circumstances the most appropriate response may be the collection of further information and monitoring of trends. This is more likely to occur in relation to

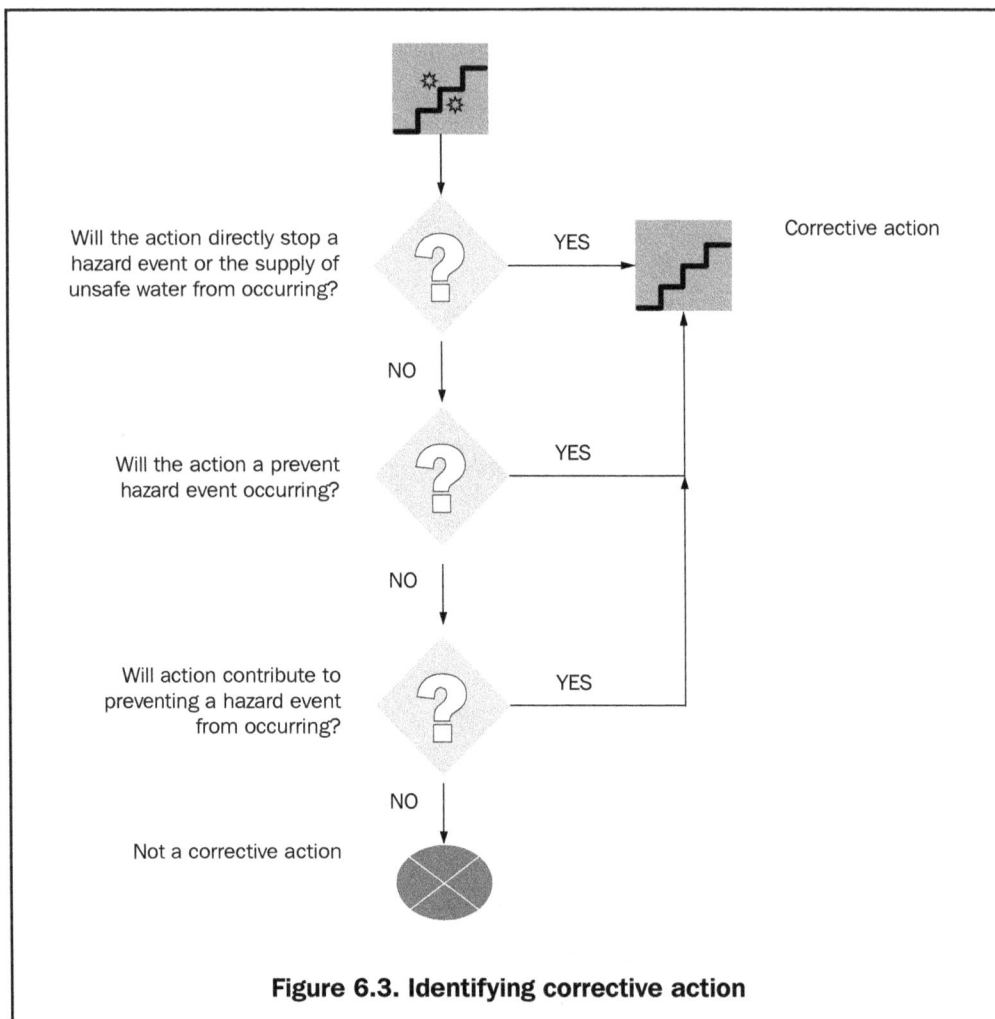

Figure 6.3. Identifying corrective action

control measures for hazards: whose impact and importance to health is uncertain; or where the pathway to the water supply is not clearly understood; and the length of time it will take the hazard to reach the water source is vague; or whether it is known if changes in concentration may have occurred. In such circumstances, it may be appropriate to include monitoring of the released hazard as a corrective action in addition to actions to prevent further release of the hazard.

Summary

At the end of this stage, a WSP matrix can be developed for each of the identified inspection points. This should begin with identification of the hazard event and end with the identification of corrective actions. This matrix can be used as the operational tool through which water quality can be managed in the system.

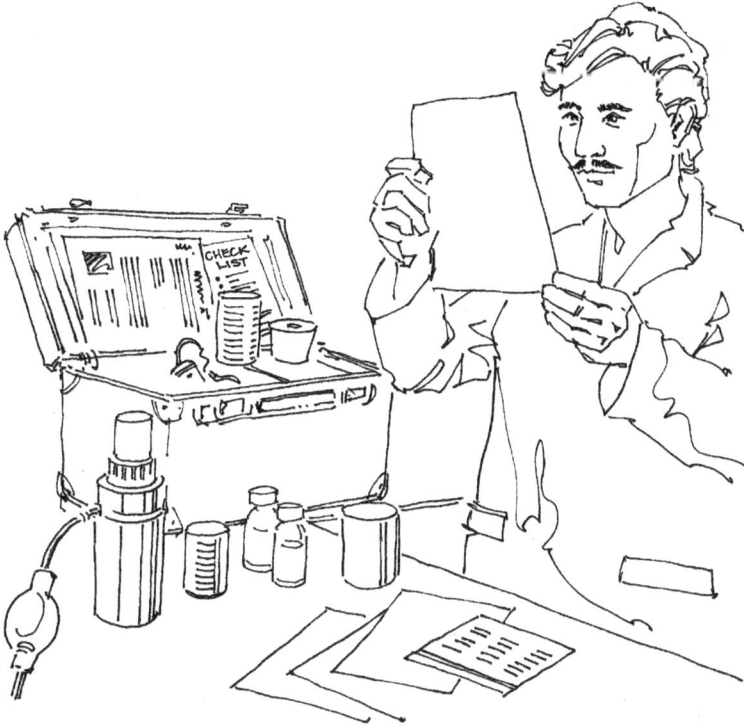

Chapter 7

Stage 6: Verification – water quality analysis

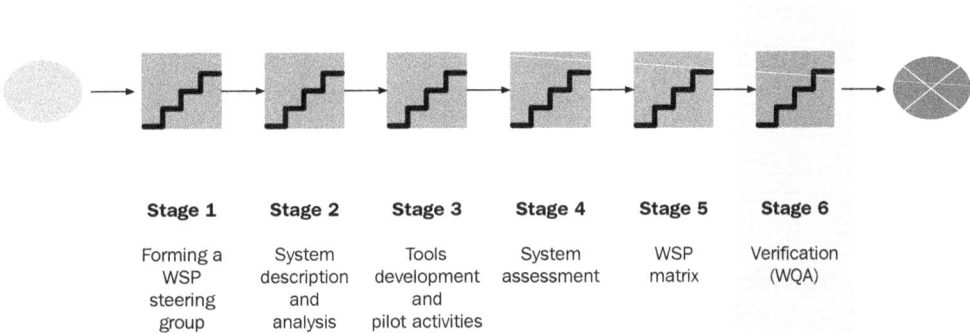

Stage 1	Stage 2	Stage 3	Stage 4	Stage 5	Stage 6
Forming a WSP steering group	System description and analysis	Tools development and pilot activities	System assessment	WSP matrix	Verification (WQA)

Analysing water quality is one way to periodically verify whether the WSP is able to ensure compliance with water quality targets or not (see further documents in this series). This should not be interpreted as an invitation to simply maintain the existing use of microbiological indicators, as their use is not related to routine operational control, but rather periodic assessment. Verification is the way to confirm that the WSP is providing water that meets the targets established for safe drinking-water. Verification typically involves operational audits (including physical inspection) and analysis of index/indicator micro-organisms and chemicals. Verification should be carried out periodically, and for piped water systems this is likely to involve a regular rolling programme of analysis, inspection and audit of water supplies.

Operational audits should include the systematic review of operational procedures and documentation to ensure that the WSP is used and that all actions required to maintain safety controls have been followed. During the audit the operations records of all treatment processes and distribution system maintenance should be reviewed to assess whether they reflect the requirements for each component of the system: outlined in both the WSP and the guidance documentation for the system. Spot checks in the field should also be carried out. The audit team should travel with the operations staff and watch them perform the tasks required under the WSP. These tasks will include: checking the frequency and efficiency of filter back-washing; checking the dosing of chlorine and routine maintenance; and cleaning of the distribution system. A key element of the audit process is to identify what operational shortcomings may be at fault when monitoring results deviate from the critical limits. The audit should identify both shortcomings in the overall WSP and modifications and improvements required.

Microbial analysis

In order for both the verification of the WSP and control measures using microbiological analysis to be effective, a range of organisms will be required. It is important that the purpose of using particular organisms is understood, to help interpret the findings.

- **Process indicators**: refer to organisms that are analysed because they indicate how well treatment processes are operating. A good example is sulphate-reducing *clostridia*. This is a spore-forming bacteria and can be used to assess treatment performance and act as a partial surrogate for protozoa.
- **Faecal indicators**: refer to organisms whose presence indicates faecal contamination. This includes bacteria such as *E.coli*, thermotolerant coliforms and faecal *streptococci*.

- **Index or model organism**: are organisms that indicate pathogen behaviour (and in some cases presence). This group includes coliphages as models of virus behaviour.

The classification is important to bear in mind when interpreting the findings of the analysis of micro-organisms. The presence of process indicators after treatment implies that the process(es) are not working properly and that there is a risk of pathogen breakthrough. They do not prove that pathogens are present, but do show whether the processes designed to remove them are functioning properly. The presence of faecal indicator organisms can indicate that either the treatment processes are not working at an optimal level or that ingress may have occurred. Pathogens may still be present. This suggests that the WSP is not working correctly and that investigations are required to improve WSP implementation. Crucially, the presence or absence of these organisms does not in itself describe safety which must be interpreted in light of other assessments.

The testing of microbes should be carried out throughout the treatment works and in the distribution systems. It is recommended that sulphite-reducing *clostridia* are used for treatment works as the resistance to chemical disinfection is similar to protozoa. As they are smaller than most protozoa their removal would also ensure that all protozoa are removed. Analysis of sulphite-reducing clostridia is not recommended in the distribution system: their presence will be difficult to interpret. These are environmentally robust organisms and their presence in the distribution system could reflect very old or very recent contamination. It will also be unclear whether their presence resulted from treatment failure or ingress within the distribution.

E.coli and faecal *streptococci* should be used at the treatment works (where their role will be primarily as process indicators) and in the distribution system (where they will be primarily used as faecal indicators). Bacteriophages (particularly somatic coliphages) can also be analysed throughout the system. In the treatment works it will function primarily as a process indicator were it provides evidence of whether viral removal is likely to be effective. In both the treatment works and the distribution system, the presence of bacteriophages will indicate the likely presence of pathogenic viruses.

Chemical analysis

In addition to microbial analysis, chemical analysis will be required during verification. The selection of chemical parameters will depend on which chemical hazards were identified as being present during the hazard assessment. If the hazard was identified as being in the source water, analysis may be undertaken either to check trends, or, if treatment is being applied, to ensure removal occurs at the correct level.

If the chemical hazard is introduced during treatment, one of two strategies can be employed. If there is concern that there may be residual levels of the hazard present even after dosing, then, analysis may be undertaken for the substance itself (an obvious example being residual aluminium). If, however, the problem is associated with impurities in the treatment chemical (e.g. alum contaminated by lead), then it is more effective to request that the supplier of the product provide quality control data.

Two particular chemical hazards will depend on the age and materials used in the distribution system: copper and lead. Copper is sometimes derived from pipes used in household plumbing systems and there will be an increased risk of copper presence with acidic waters. Lead may also be present from lead pipes or solders. Copper is most effectively verified through analysis. Verification for lead is more problematic. In cases where this is derived from pipes directly, the verification should focus on monitoring the numbers of lead pipes replaced. Where it is derived from solders, verification may require both water quality analysis and monitoring the use of solders.

Within distribution systems, if a particular source of chemical hazard has been identified then verification should include analysis of the chemical hazard expected to be present. For example, distribution systems that could be inundated by surface water bodies that receive effluent from small-scale tanneries, should be tested for chromium.

Designing a sampling network for water quality analysis in verification

The water quality analysis will be undertaken at the treatment works to verify performance, and through the distribution works. Verification works should be undertaken using two mechanisms:

- Assessments;
- rolling programmes.

In assessments, a relatively large number of samples will be taken to analyse the microbial indicators, turbidity, chlorine residuals, pH and any chemical substances identified as important. Sanitary inspections will also be performed at the same time. Samples will be taken from raw waters and the outlets of each treatment process unit to assess the performance of each process in improving water quality. Intensive assessments are designed to provide one-off cross-sectional surveys of the system performance. These assessments would be combined with a detailed operational audit (as determined by inspection of infrastructure and a review of operational records and documentation related to the WSP).

Assessments at treatment works will use the full range of process and faecal indicator organisms identified earlier and may also include index organisms. For treatment works, the assessments will require repeated sampling and analysis of the water after each unit process over a period of several days. In Uganda, for instance, this was done over three days. The assessment of water as it passes through the treatment works should also be supported by an analysis of the water within the distribution system to assess what changes are expected as the water moves through the whole supply. Sample points should include all major primary and secondary infrastructure (service reservoirs, major valves) and a sample of tertiary infrastructure.

Where there is a hydraulic model of the system, planning of the timing and location of the sampling points in the supply should be determined by estimating the amount of time it would take for water to reach different parts of the system. In this way, the water can be tracked as it passes through the supply and a more accurate picture of deterioration in water quality developed. If such a model does not exist, then on each day of sampling at the treatment works, samples should be taken from different elements of the primary and secondary major infrastructure and a sample of tertiary infrastructure.

Rolling programme

A rolling programme of verification should also be developed that operates in a complementary fashion to the operational monitoring programme. Where there is a well-developed surveillance body, the rolling programme of verification may be fully delegated to the surveillance function. Where this is not the case, or where a more audit-based approach to surveillance is implemented, the water supplier will be responsible for ensuring these forms of verification are performed.

In rolling programmes of verification, the main emphasis is likely to be on a single or very limited range of microbial indicators. It is likely that the majority of tests will be for *E.coli*. The design of the sampling network for water quality analysis performed as part of the verification exercise needs to balance both the need for representative samples to be taken and the cost. Although it is desirable that

Box 7.1. Sample numbers by population

Population	Number of samples per month
Below 5000	3 samples per month (source/treatment works plus 2 in distribution)
5000 - 100,000	3 samples plus 1 extra sample per 5000 extra people
Above 100,000	1 sample per 10,000 people plus 10 samples

sampling programmes be designed on a statistical basis, this is not often feasible, as the number of samples required is very high. WHO suggest a population-based approach to sampling as shown in Box 7.1.

Documentation

The final stage of developing the WSP is to prepare a set of documents that describe how water safety will be maintained in the supply. This would typically include:

- risk assessments performed on the supply;
- the water safety plan itself;
- standard operating procedures (SOPs) for analyses for operational monitoring and verification;
- SOPs for sanitary inspections;
- data on validation;
- lines of reporting and communication with the public;
- results of operational monitoring;
- results of verification; and
- details of all corrective actions undertaken.

Documentation should be stored in the risk manager's office with copies distributed as appropriate. Documentation should be updated regularly as improvements are made to the WSP and associated activities. Furthermore, public annual water safety reports should be prepared to promote transparency and accountability within water safety management.

Chapter 8

Using the WSP

Once each of the development stages of the WSP has been followed and a WSP has been established, it should be used as the primary tool for water safety management in the water supply. Therefore it is an operational tool to support water safety management and should form the basis of workload planning for relevant staff. Ultimately, the risk manager should take overall responsibility for managing the water safety plan. This will include: ensuring that all the required monitoring is performed; action taking and notification of key staff when critical limits are exceeded; planning and overseeing the verification plan; ensuring that all data are stored appropriately; prepare and submit reports as required; planning and implementing a system of internal audit of water supplies with WSPs; and undertaking periodic validation exercises.

It is extremely important that these systems are established and followed if water safety management is to be implemented effectively. The systems referred to here mean the procedures by which information is shared and acted upon by both different departments within the utility and external stakeholders. An example of

---

Box 8.1. Operationalization of WSP – an example from Uganda

Following three years of research of the application of WSPs in Uganda, NWSC decided to implement a WSP in both Kampala and Jinja. The operationalization of the WSP has taken different forms. In Kampala, NWSC have invested substantial funds to upgrade the system by rehabilitating principle infrastructure as well as installing sampling taps for all the control points. In Jinja, NWSC have increased their frequency of monitoring of the control points and developed a comprehensive monitoring and verification plan. As the Managing Director of NWSC said "the advantage of the WSP is that it provides a system for managers and operators to work together to understand their water supply more effectively."

---

the operationalization of a WSP can be found in National Water and Sewerage (NWSC) Water Safety Plans (WSP) Operational Manual, Kampala, Uganda (NWSC et al., 2003).

Communication

The lines of communication and reporting that are required throughout the WSP process are vitally important. This is a challenge for both the 'risk sector' and the water supply sector. It is important to identifying: who in the water supply organization will be notified of the problem when it occurs; which other people will be notified and advised; and which internal and external groups will be notified when the problem is rectified (Lang et al., 2001) (see Box 8.2). Lang et al. (2001), suggest that normally either the operations staff or water quality control staff would be the first to identify if a problem had occurred, either through their regular inspections and work on the system or because of customer complaints. Minor problems should be reported to the risk manager to instigate corrective action on the system, and only when major problems are recorded should the operations manager be informed. This will streamline the reporting process and ensure that appropriate action is taken. The risk manager should also be responsible for: deciding whether wider notification is required; what additional actions may be needed to avoid supply of unsafe water; and who should mobilize water quality control staff to undertake the necessary analysis of water.

Effective and timely communication between the monitoring and management sections of the utility should occur routinely as part of monitoring activities, and is essential when critical limits have been exceeded and action is required. This allows a number of key actions to be addressed and incorporated into the field implementation:

- Ensure that all members of the utility know which departments are responsible for key tasks regarding the WSP (e.g., monitoring, verification, operational control, approval of additional works, etc.).
- Nominate responsible staff members to ensure that information is passed between monitoring and management sections. This should clearly identify who within the organization should transmit information, who should receive it directly and who should receive copies.
- Establish a written agreed reporting procedure for the transfer of information both when control measures exceed critical limits and when they are in compliance. One utility in Australia which adopted HACCP plans for their water supplies, automatically sends emails to senior staff whenever a critical limit is exceeded. This has improved the timeliness of responses and ensures that more direct management involvement is sustained.

Box 8.2. Communication strategies

Severity of hazard event	Operations manager	Risk manager	Senior management	Regulator/ health body	Consumers
Catastrophic	Must be informed immediately	Must be informed immediately	Informed immediately by risk manager	Informed immediately by risk manager	Advised immediately on necessary action approved by risk manager
Minor	Must only be informed if problem persists	Must be informed immediately	Informed only if problem persists	Informed only if problem persists	Advised immediately on necessary action approved by risk manager

- Notify relevant people when corrective action has been completed - it is necessary to outline when this information should be provided, and by whom, and who within the organization should be informed.
- Confirm adequacy of corrective actions - this should clearly define how rapidly the monitoring section will visit and test the control measures following the corrective action.

Communication within organizations is often poor and fails to deliver expected actions. In some utilities, the relationship between the monitoring and operations department is rather antagonistic: the operations department views the monitoring department as some kind of 'policing' body that is only concerned with identifying failures and inadequacies.

These problems may be overcome by two processes at the core of the WSP approach:

- The use of multi-disciplinary teams in developing the WSP – this makes subsequent inter-departmental collaboration easier as roles, responsibilities and required interactions are more clearly defined.
- Feedback – the monitoring department provides feedback to the operations department and managers when the outcomes of monitoring and verification are good, as well as when failures are noted. Developing systematic reporting mechanisms, including regular meetings where possible, is essential in strengthening the implementation of the WSP. These may also provide opportunities for improvement in the WSP and in building trust between the different departments.

Operations departments are typically more powerful than monitoring departments and this may mean that the monitoring process and the use of the results are not taken seriously enough to improve the supply. The inter-disciplinary nature of WSPs should offer an opportunity to overcome these problems by highlighting the benefit to the operations department of effective and focused monitoring activities. Ensuring that there is acceptance of the need for monitoring and the use of results to make improvements when required, also forms part of the prerequisites of institutional commitment to water safety.

Internal communication can be facilitated by establishing a regular system of information sharing (via reports provided on a weekly basis and after incidents) supported by regular meetings (preferably monthly) to discuss water safety and annual reviews of the WSP. This should be co-ordinated by the risk manager.

Operational monitoring

The monitoring plan provides the water quality and operations staff with a framework for their routine monitoring activities at the treatment works and within the distribution system. It should: include a detailed description of all the points within the water supply where monitoring will be undertaken; show how often monitoring will be performed; and by whom.

The water safety manager should ensure that this plan is followed by the appropriate staff. Where the monitoring will be performed by staff within the water quality/ safety management department, the water safety manager should review monthly and annual work plans to ensure that these reflect the monitoring requirements of the WSP. The water safety manager should also review the reports prepared by the monitoring teams to ensure that an adequate level of activity has been maintained and that all cases where critical limits were exceeded have been reported and appropriate action taken.

It is also important to consider how to establish systems to ensure that any incident where a critical limit is exceeded is rapidly detected. This is particularly important at points where the impact of failure entails a high risk, for instance failure in treatment or in a major service reservoir. Many utilities in developed countries have installed on-line chlorine monitors that trip an alarm and may cut the supply when the free chlorine drops below the required concentration. Although often considered too expensive in developing countries, on larger water supplies such equipment may be affordable and given the likely impact on very large numbers of people, may result in significant health protection. The costs of the alternative approach (a staff member to regularly test water manually) should also be considered and a cost-benefit analysis performed. It is unlikely, however, that systems used in developed countries with remote telemetry fitted to alarms will be feasible, in part because it may be difficult to guarantee that action to repair the fault with the chlorine dosing will be repaired within a very short time frame, which is essential to support such approaches. Box A1.4 (see Annexe 1) outlines selected monitoring points.

Who should do the monitoring?

The identification of appropriate personnel to perform monitoring functions is a critical component of implementing the WSP. Different types of monitoring may be undertaken by different members of staff. It is therefore essential that the water safety manager, or a staff member reporting to the water safety manager, coordinates activities properly: ensuring that there is a central record of all results; and a clear overview of all monitoring which has been undertaken. As some monitoring is likely to be performed by staff in the operations departments, the water safety manager will also need to liaise with other departments.

At water treatment works the monitoring will be most appropriately performed by the water treatment plant operators, as they will be based at the treatment works and will be able to perform the frequent, routine monitoring likely to be required. Staff operating water treatment works are sometimes within an operations department and sometimes within a water quality department. If the treatment works is under the remit of the operations department, it is important that systems are established to ensure the routine reporting of results to the risk manager. This may be a daily routine transfer of results with immediate notification of failures, when these occur.

It may be cost effective to delegate monitoring in the distribution system to operations staff as part of their routine work at key points within the distribution system, for instance service reservoirs. In many ways this would be the preferred option as corrective actions needed when critical limits are exceeded are likely to be the responsibility of the operations department. Where this approach is followed, it is essential that records from all monitoring are passed to the water quality/safety manager to ensure that a complete record is maintained.

In the distribution system there will be some fixed points for monitoring, usually at service reservoirs and major valves. At these sites, monitoring would be expected to be daily, weekly or at least monthly. Some less important valves may receive monitoring on a quarterly basis. Within the tertiary infrastructure, sampling will be on the basis of a rolling programme of visits throughout the system. The aim being: to gain a clear understanding of recurrent and persistent problems; and to develop programmes that reduce risks.

Corrective actions

Corrective actions will primarily be the responsibility of the treatment plant operators and the distribution operations department. It is therefore essential that corrective actions identified for control measures are agreed between the water safety management department and the operations department. Without agreement, it may be difficult to ensure that actions are taken when they are required.

Planning for corrective actions will require that the operations department identify staff in different parts of the system who will be responsible for responding to incidents and undertaking corrective actions. In some utilities, no differentiation is made between routine and response work, and where incidents are rare, this is the most cost effective approach to ensure that staff time is used efficiently. In utilities where critical limits are often exceeded, the utility may establish a team of staff identified to respond to emergencies in addition to the team undertaking routine operation and maintenance work. In these cases, it is likely that the staff will rotate, with some time spent in routine operation and maintenance and some in the response team.

The operations department should ensure that the appropriate tools and materials are readily available to carry out corrective actions, and that on completion of the required work, the water quality department are notified to verify water safety. Records of actions taken should be kept and brief reports prepared for the management and water safety management department. Planning for corrective action should include establishing guidelines or targets for the speed of response to an incident. This often becomes a useful tool for monitoring performance and promoting the utility amongst its existing and potential customers by demonstrating good practice.

When work is undertaken on distribution systems, both as part of corrective actions and during routine operation and maintenance, it is essential that a code of practice for hygienic working is established. This typically includes ensuring that all materials used in the distribution system are kept clean, that vehicles are never used in wastewater systems, that staff are not allowed to directly work on the distribution system if they have been working on the wastewater system, and that sanitation facilities are available for staff on-site. Some utilities also require that staff both inform other staff if they have had a water-related infectious disease (which may prevent them working on the distribution system) and have regular medical checks. Many utilities prepare simplified codes of practice which are given to staff and are put into every vehicle used for work in the distribution system. This provides staff with a constant reference point to ensure that hygienic working practices are always followed.

Verification plan

Verification may be undertaken by the department within the utility responsible for water quality or water safety, or by an external laboratory contracted by the utility to undertake this work. In some situations, verification may be performed by a mixture of approaches, with some testing by the utility and an external contracted laboratory carrying out other analyses.

The risk manager should be responsible for ensuring that the verification programme is properly planned: the required number of samples being taken at the appropriate sample sites. It is likely that, like the monitoring programme, there will be a mixture of fixed and variable sampling sites. The detail of each sampling round should be prepared by the teams responsible for staff undertaking the sampling and analysis in the field, and approved by the water safety manager. All data should be kept on a database and regular reports prepared.

Verification in the distribution system will be an ongoing rolling programme involving monthly testing. Verification at the treatment works for *E.coli* will also be ongoing, with regular tests performed on raw and finished water as part of the overall monthly verification plan. Additional exercises may be considered for treatment works on a periodic basis to analyse a wider range of organisms. For instance, there may be a quarterly programme of verification using sulphite-reducing *clostridia* or coliphage.

In addition to analysis of water quality, verification should also entail an audit of the WSP and of operational practice as a means of demonstrating compliance with good practice. It is useful to use internal as well as external audits, although the latter is a requirement if formal registration with a management system (such as HACCP or ISO) is followed.

Davison et al., (2004) outline in some detail the information that should be obtained when undertaking an audit or reviewing a WSP. The basic purpose of reviewing the WSP is to ensure that the team preparing and/or implementing the WSP have:

- taken all feasible hazard events into account;
- identified appropriate control measures for each event;
- established how the measures will be monitored;
- established critical limits for each control measure;
- identified a corrective action when critical limits have been exceeded; and
- set up a system of verification.

It is expected that most WSPs will be iterative and will undergo regular updating and improvement, as both the understanding of the system improves and investments are made. Therefore regular review and update of WSPs for individual supplies should be built into the work plans of the water safety team.

Conclusions

This document has outlined the six main stages in developing a Water Safety Plan. In line with the revised 3rd edition of the World Health Organisation *Guidelines for Drinking-Water Quality* (WHO, 2004), the Water Safety Plan approach is the recommended means of assuring water quality in piped urban systems. It has covered a number of key areas of importance in developing WSPs: the need for

Box 8.3. Verification plan – Jinja, Uganda

Unit process	Monitoring			Verification		
	What	When	Who	What	When	Who
Treatment works						
Coagulation/ flocculation	On line measurement – pH	Daily	Analyst	E. coli	Weekly	Analyst
	Jar testing records	Weekly	Water	Faecal streptococci	Weekly	
	Turbidity	Daily	Treatment	Record audit	Monthly	
	Dosing records	Monthly	Operators			
Distribution system	pH	Weekly	Analyst	E. coli	Monthly	Analyst
	Turbidity	Weekly		Faecal streptococci	Monthly	
	Cl$_2$	Weekly				
	Sanitary inspection	Weekly				

an interdisciplinary team to manage the WSP development; the development of WSPs in the absence of detailed data or maps of the supply; and the importance of increased monitoring and decreased verification in light of the logistical and financial constraints facing water utilities in the developing world.

Chapter 9

References

Bartram, J., Fewtrell, L., Stenstrom, T-A. (2001) 'Harmonised assessment of risk and risk management for water-related infectious disease: an overview' in Fewtrell, L. and Bartram, J. *Water Quality: Guidelines, Standards and Health: Assessment of Risk and Risk Management for Water-Related Infectious Disease*, WHO, Geneva, pp.1-17.

Davison, A., Howard, G., Stevens, M., Fewtrell, L., Deere., D, Callan, P., Bartram, J. (2004) *Water Safety Plans*, WHO, Geneva.

Deere, D., Stevens, M., Davison, A., Helm, G., Dufour, A. (2001) 'Management Strategies', in Fewtrell, L. and Bartram, J., *Water Quality: Guidelines, Standards and Health: Assessment of Risk and Risk Management for Water-Related Infectious Disease*, WHO, Geneva, pp. 257-289.

Dillon, M. and Griffith, C. (1996) *How to HACCP*, 2nd Edition, MD Associates, Grimsby, UK.

DFID. (1998). *Guidance Manual for Water Supply and Sanitation Programmes*, WELL, London, UK.

Godfrey, S., Niwagaba, C., Howard, G., and Tibatemwa, S. (2002), *Water Safety Plans for Developing Countries – A Case Study from Kampala*, Uganda, WEDC, UK.

Havelaar, A. and Melse, V., (2003) *'Quantifying Public Health Risk' in the WHO Guidelines for Drinking-Water Quality – A Burden of Disease Approach,'* RIVM Report, Netherlands.

Howard, G., (2001) Bartram, J., (2005) Effective Water Surveillance in Urban Areas of Developing Countries, *Journal of Water and Health*, Vol 3, pp. 31-43

Howard, G., (2002) *Water Supply Surveillance – A Reference Manual*, WEDC, UK.

Howard, G. and Bartram J. (in press) *'Effective Approaches to Water Supply Surveillance in Urban Areas of Developing Countries.'* Water and Health., IWA Publications, UK.

Lang, S., Fewtrell, L. and Bartram, J. (2001) 'Risk Communication,' in Bartram, J. and Fewtrell, L., *Water Quality: Guidelines, Standards and Health: Assessment of Risk and Risk Management for Water-Related Infectious Disease*, WHO, Geneva, pp.317-33.

LeChevallier, M. and Au, K-K., (2003) *Impact of Treatment on Microbial Water Quality: A Review Document on Treatment Efficiency to Remove Pathogens*, WHO, Geneva.

Medema, G. J., Payment, P., Dufour, A., Robertson, W., Waite, M., Hunter, P., Kirby, R. and Anderson, Y. (2003) 'Safe Drinking-Water: An Ongoing Challenge' in Fewtrell, L. (ed), *Assessing Microbial Safety of Drinking-Water - Improving Approaches and Methods*, IWA, London.

National Water and Sewerage (NWSC), 'GIS Mapping Section/Operations (OSUL), PHEE, Makerere University,' in Godfrey, S. and Howard, G. (2003) *Water Safety Plans (WSP) Operational Manual, Kampala*, Uganda, WEDC, UK.

New Zealand Ministry of Health (NZMOH) (2001) *Public Health Risk Management Plan Guide*, New Zealand.

Payment, P. (1998) *'Distribution Impact on Microbial Disease'*, Water Supply, 16 (3-4), pp. 113-119.

Prem Chand, Anwar, M., Rao, C., V., Kumar, R., and Godfrey S. (2003) *'Water Safety Plans for Utilities in Developing Countries – A Case Study from Guntur, India.'* KAKTOS, Guntur, India.

Tibatemwa, S., Godfrey, S., Nabasurye, L. and Niwagaba, C. (2003) *Water Safety Plans for Utilities in Developing Countries - A Case Study from Jinja, Uganda*, WEDC, UK.

World Health Organization (1997) *Guidelines for Drinking-Water Quality*, Volume 3: Surveillance and Control of Community Supplies, 2nd edition, Geneva.

World Health Organization (2004) *Guidelines for Drinking-Water Quality*, Volume 1: Recommendations, 3rd edition, Geneva.

Annexes

Annexe 1: Additional boxes

Annexe 2: Case study examples

Annexe 3: Sanitary inspection forms

Annexe 1: Additional boxes

Box A1.1. Mapping piped systems when no map was available – Guntur, India

Data collection on piped systems is very difficult where there are few available maps. For example in Guntur, the only available maps were 25 years old and were of the road network. There were **no** water network maps available.

To overcome this difficulty KAKTOS Consult. in collaboration with the Public Health Engineering Department and Guntur Municipal Council (GMC) developed the following methodology:

- Use road map as basis
- Conduct a road network survey for roads built within last 25 years
- Using the road as a reference, mark the boundaries of the administrative zones
- By zone, using expert judgement, identify the approximate location of the water treatment works and supply tanks
- Mark the primary pipeline on road map from treatment works to tanks
- Define diameter of primary/secondary mains (Guntur - >200mm = primary main)
- Use field validation to locate secondary pipelines and major valves
- Prepare a map using either tracing paper or computerized digitisation
- Divide the map into blocks (in Guntur each block = 0.5km²)

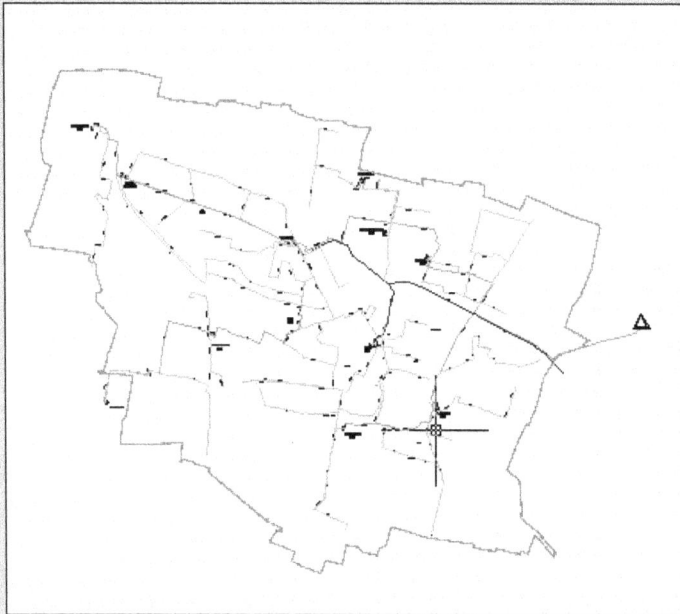

Map of Guntur Pipelines (Prem Chand et al., 2003)

Box A1.2. Zoning with data - Example from Kampala, Uganda

In the Kampala system, a total of six major supply zones were identified based on the service reservoirs. The zones were demarcated on a pipe network map of the system through hydraulic mapping by the operations managers and engineers. During the mapping process, the supply patterns from the two Kampala water treatment works (Gaba 1 and Gaba 2) to the service reservoirs were marked along with connections on the high and low-pressure transmissions mains. From each of the supplied service reservoirs water movement was then traced using block maps. Major isolation valves, cut off points or points of potential mixing were marked.

Within these six zones there are 22 sub zones, each with its own discrete area of supply. These are mostly defined by separate booster stations and/or supply tanks. Although these sub zones are important as a tool in the management of individual components of the system, it should be emphasized that the foundation of the system lies in the six main supply zones. From a water quality perspective, it is these six zones that are key to the understanding of contaminant dispersal and movement throughout the system.

Source: (Godfrey et al., 2002)

Box A1.3. Zoning without data – an example from Jinja, Uganda

The network has no hydraulic model and limited available data. To identify the supply zones, the primary and secondary mains were identified (blue and yellow respectively) on paper copies of maps. Three zones were then demarcated: low level (red), high level (yellow) and booster tank (green). The extremes of these zones were plotted as an overlay on the map on tracing paper. These were divided according to the location of the isolation valves.

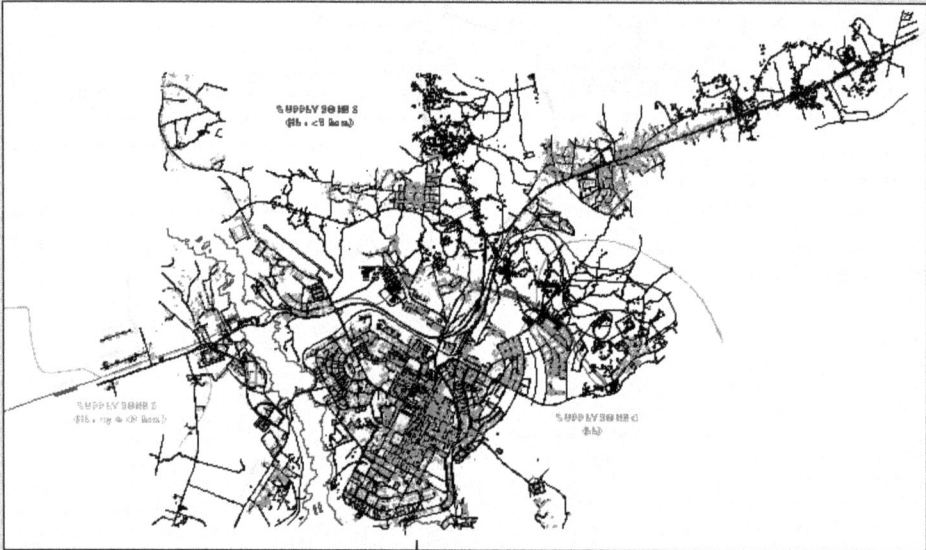

Source: (Tibatemwa et al., 2003)

Box A1.4. Monitoring plan Kampala, Uganda

The map indicates the identified monitoring points for Kampala. These include treatment works, primary valves, secondary valves, supply tanks, service reservoirs and randomly selected standpipes.

The monthly frequency of monitoring for each of these sampling points to be recommended in Kampala was:

- Water treatment works = 2x per week
- Service reservoirs = 2x per week
- Supply tanks = 1x per week
- Primary valves = 1x per week
- Secondary valves = 1x per month
- Tertiary standpipes = 1x per month

Annexe 2: Case study examples

Activity	Kampala	Jinja	Guntur
Step 1: Forming the team	System is managed through private lease contract between the government run by NWSC and ONDEO Uganda Services Ltd (OSUL). Representatives from both were members of an interdisciplinary WSP steering group.	NWSC is responsible for both production and distribution of the water. A steering committee was formed that comprised only of NWSC staff and not staff from private operators. The team was coordinated by the Area Engineer assigned the role of Risk Manager.	Guntur is located in the state of Andrapradesh, India. The water supply system supplies 75,000m³ per day through approximately 600km of pipeline The system is operated by the Guntur Municipal Corporation (GMC). Water quality is monitored in isolation by tap inspectors from The Public Health Engineering Department (PHE).
Step 2: System Analysis	System is fed from a surface water source in Lake Victoria to two treatment works following conventional treatment unit processes. The combined capacity of the works is 95,000m³/day, which is then distributed to five major service reservoirs. There are two distinct pressure zones (high and low) in the supply. No hydraulic model exists for the supply but 0.5km² block maps are available for the entire supply area. Total of 182 risk points identified.	System is fed from a surface water source from the Napolean Gulf of Lake Victoria to one treatment works following conventional treatment unit processes. The operational capacity of the works is 26,000m³/day, which is then distributed to two major service reservoirs. There are two distinct pressure zones (high and low) and three supply zones identified using 'expert judgement' or local knowledge of the supply.	No system maps existed for Guntur. Innovative approaches such as semi qualitative risk mapping were therefore used. A total of 206 points were identified throughout the system
Step 3: Development of tools	Two sanitary inspection tools used: Assessment tools used infrequently to assess the sanitary integrity of the system and Monitoring tools designed to be used on regular basis to monitor the sanitary integrity of specific points with in the system. Standardization of questions in these tools was critical for comparing risk.	As in Kampala	As in Kampala

Activity	Kampala	Jinja	Guntur
Step 4: System Assessment	Total of 152 inspection points were assessed using sanitary inspections and selected physico chemical analysis. Based on results of the assessment 82 high risk control points were identified.	Total of 46 points were identified throughout the system. They included 35 in high level pressure zones and 11 in low level pressure zones. A team of three people worked took three days to complete the assessment. Between 10 and 15 inspection points were assessed per day.	After discussion all the buried valve boxes, road crosses with no available data were removed Removal of these points made the total number of inspection points through out the system is 163, a very high number for a 600km system. From the initial 163 points, 62 control points were identified.
Step 5: Water Safety Plan matrix	WSP matrices were then developed for each point.	As in Kampala based on sanitary inspection	As in Kampala based on Sanitary inspection
Step 6: Verification	Two assessments were done, one before the launch of the WSP and one six months later. Samples were taken at the water treatment works and at 50 of the 82 identified control points. Samples were tested for sulphate reducing *clostridia*, faecal *streptococci* and thermotolerant coliforms.	The initial exercise showed that the Jinja system is generally of good sanitary integrity. The level of sanitary risks identified at the service reservoirs and tanks were low at 10% risk. Major problems were corrosion inside the metal tanks, and uncovered vents	System indicated very high levels of microbial contamination. Findings from the system assessment indicated average pH levels of 6-7, turbidity of 5-7NTU and variable residual chlorine levels. During the microbial verification exercise, 52 control points were sampled.
Results and Recommendations	The assessments revealed relatively low levels of microbial contamination in the Kampala system suggesting that it was a well run supply. Findings from the system assessment revealed low (or non existent) levels of residual chlorine suggesting either excessive absorption of chlorine into biofilm and/or leakage/ingress of contaminated water in supply. High sanitary risks were identified in service reservoirs, supply tanks and major valves. Control points identified at major valves required upgrading of valve boxes and installation of sampling taps to enable access for water sample collection.	The Jinja system is a relatively small supply with few control points. Findings indicated high levels of contamination in low lying areas as valve boxes were submerged. Recommendations included weekly monitoring of each of the 30 control points once per week. This will mean a total of 30 x 4 weeks per month (Total 120 per month). Verification will include approximately 30 samples per month.	Findings indicated high additional dosing of bleach at the outlet of the service reservoirs. Limited correlation was found between high levels of chlorine and high microbial contamination.

Annexe 3: Sanitary inspection forms

Type of facility **_PRIMARY MAINS_**

1. General information: Zone: Area:
2. Code number
3. Date of visit
4. Water samples taken? Sample No.

Specific diagnostic information for assessment

(Please indicate at which sites the risk was identified) **Risk Sample No.**

1. Is there any evidence of leakage? Y/N
2. Is there any evidence of human faeces in vicinity of pipe? Y/N
3. Are there animal faeces in the vicinity of the pipe? Y/N
4. Does the primary main pass through stagnant water? Y/N
5. Is there any evidence of solid waste in the vicinity of the pipe? Y/N
6. Is there any evidence of excessive algal growth in proximity of the pipe?Y/N
7. Is there any evidence of a primary line crossing culvert? Y/N
8. Are there any air valves connected to the standpipe? Y/N

Risk score: 6-8 = Very high; 5-7 = High; 3-4 = Medium; 0-3 = Low

Results and recommendations

The following important points of risk were noted: (list Nos: 1-8)

Signature of health inspectors/assistant:

Comments:

Type of facility   *SERVICE RESERVOIR*

1. General information: Zone: Area:
2. Code number
3. Date of visit:
4. Water samples taken?   Sample No.

Specific diagnostic information for assessment

(Please indicate at which sites the risk was identified)   **Risk Sample No.**

1. Are vents not covered? (could animals or birds get into the reservoir)   Y/N
2. Is the inspection cover or concrete around cover damaged or corroded?   Y/N
3. Is the inspection cover not in place when inspected?   Y/N
4. Is any observable part of the inside of the tank corroded or damaged?   Y/N
   (including ladders, roof struts, walls)
5. Is there evidence of leakage/cracks in the reservoir?   Y/N
   (check the outside of the tank to look for faults)
6. Can run-off form stagnant pools close to the reservoir?   Y/N
7. Can stagnant or dirty water collect in valve boxes or
   washout chambers? (i.e. no or blocked washout chamber)   Y/N
8. Is the reservoir unfenced or insecure?   Y/N
9. Is there evidence of faecal material surrounding the valve box?   Y/N
10. Has the tank not been cleaned within one month?   Y/N
11. Is the valve in the power house leaking?   Y/N

Risk score: 10-12 = Very high; 7-9 = High; 4-6 = Medium; 0-3 = Low

Results and recommendations

The following important points of risk were noted: (list Nos: 1-11)

Signature of Inspector:

Type of facility   *BOOSTER STATIONS*

1. General information: Zone: Area:

2. Code number

3. Date of visit

4. Water samples taken?   Sample No.

Specific diagnostic information for assessment

(Please indicate at which sites the risk was identified)   **Risk Sample No.**

1. Is the bleaching added to the water in the booster?   Y/N

2. Is any observable part of the inside of the booster corroded or damaged? Y/N
   (Including ladders, roof struts, walls)

3. Is there evidence of leakage/cracks in the booster?   Y/N
   (Check the inside of the booster to look for faults)

4. Can run-off form stagnant pools close to the booster?   Y/N

5. Can stagnant or dirty water collect in valve boxes?   Y/N

6. Is the booster unfenced or insecure?   Y/N

7. Is there evidence of faecal material surrounding the valve box?   Y/N

8. Has the booster not been cleaned within one month?   Y/N

9. Is the valve in the powerhouse leaking?   Y/N

Risk score: 9-10 = Very high; 6-8 = High; 3-5 = Medium; 0-3 = Low

Results and recommendations

The following important points of risk were noted: (list Nos: 1-9)

Signature of Inspector:

Comments:

Type of facility   *VALVE BOXES*

1. General information: Zone: Area:

2. Code number

3. Date of visit

4. Water samples taken?   Sample No.

Specific diagnostic information for assessment

(Please indicate at which sites the risk was identified)   **Risk Sample No.**

1. Is the valve not operational?   Y/N

2. Was the cover missing when visited?   Y/N

3. Is the valve box cover cracked?   Y/N

4. Is the valve corroded?   Y/N

5. Does the valve leak?   Y/N

6. Is there a lack of backflow preventers installed on supply main?   Y/N

7. Is there debris or faecal matter in the valve box?   Y/N

8. Is the valve box designed without washout?   Y/N

9. Is there stagnant water in valve box?   Y/N

10. Are there evident standpipes connected to the valve?   Y/N

Risk score: 8-10 = Very high; 6-7 = High; 4-5 = Medium; 0-3 = Low

Results and recommendations

The following important points of risk were noted: (list Nos: 1-10)

Signature of inspectors/assistant:

Comments

Type of facility   *ROADS, DRAINS AND DITCHES*

1. General information: Zone: Area:

2. Code number

3. Date of visit

4. Water samples taken?   Sample No.

Specific diagnostic information for assessment

(Please indicate at which sites the risk was identified)   **Risk Sample No.**

1. Is there a valve box within 1m of road crossing?   Y/N

2. Is the supply pipe exposed close to the road crossing?   Y/N

3. Is there evidence of ingress into the pipe from stagnant water?   Y/N

4. Is there evidence of cattle faeces in the area surrounding of the pipe?   Y/N

5. Is there evidence of leakage around the pipe?   Y/N

6. Does pipe cross open ditch/trench?   Y/N

7. Is there evidence of faeces in trench/ditch?   Y/N

8. Is there waste material around the pipe?   Y/N

9. Is the pipe submerged in stagnant water?   Y/N

10. Is the pipe damaged/cracked/leaking/pitted?   Y/N

Risk score: 9-10 = Very high; 6-8 = High; 3-5 = Medium; 0-3 = Low

Results and recommendations

The following important points of risk were noted: (list Nos. 1-10)

Signature of Health Inspector/Assistant:

Comments:

Type of facility   *STANDPIPES/HOUSE CONNECTIONS*

1. General information: Zone: Area:

2. Code number

3. Date of visit

4. Water samples taken?   Sample No.

Specific diagnostic information for assessment

(Please indicate at which sites the risk was identified)   **Risk Sample No.**

1. Do any standpipes leak?   Y/N

2. Does surface water collect around any standpipe?   Y/N

3. Is animal faeces in the vicinity of the standpipe?   Y/N

4. Are pipes exposed close to any tap stand?   Y/N

5. Is human excreta on the ground within 10m of any standpipe?   Y/N

6. Is the main pipe submerged in stagnant water?   Y/N

7. Are there solid waste dumps 10m from tap stands?   Y/N

8. Are there stagnant pools of water close to the pipe?   Y/N

9. Does the main pipe pass through sewage/pit latrines/septic tank
   foul water bodies?   Y/N

10.Does main pipe cross a drain/ditch? (if YES go to road crossing SI)   Y/N

Risk score: 8-10 = Very high; 5-7 = High; 3-4 = Medium; 0-3 = Low

Results and recommendations

The following important points of risk were noted: (list Nos: 1-10)

Signature of health inspectors/assistant:

Comments:

Type of facility   *TREATMENT PROCESSES*

1. General information: Zone: Area:

2. Code number

3. Date of visit

4. Water samples taken?   Sample No.

Specific diagnostic information for assessment

(Please indicate at which sites the risk was identified)   **Risk Sample No.**

1. Are there evident cracks in the pre-filters?   Y/N

2. Are there leaks in the mixing tank?   Y/N

3. Is the mixing tank in an unsanitary condition?   Y/N

4. Are there evident hydraulic surges in intake?   Y/N

5. Is the sedimentation tank in an unsanitary condition?   Y/N

6. Is the air and water supply distribution in the sand bed unseen?   Y/N

7. Are there mud balls or cracks in the filters?   Y/N

8. Are there evident cross connections between backwashed and treated water?   Y/N

9. Is there evidence of insufficient alum dosing?   Y/N

10. Are insufficient Cl2 RCL levels not being achieved?   Y/N

Risk score: 8-10 = Very high; 6-7 = High; 3-5 = Medium; 0-3 = Low

Results and recommendations

The following important points of risk were noted: (list Nos. 1-10)

Signature of Health Inspector/Assistant:

Comments:

www.ingramcontent.com/pod-product-compliance
Lightning Source LLC
Chambersburg PA
CBHW080926050426
42334CB00055B/2789